LINCOLN CHRISTIAN COLLEGE AND SEMINARY

D0102783

Strategic Planning for Churches

An Appreciative Approach

Charles Elliott

Strategic Planning for Churches
An Appreciative Approach

Published by CMR Press
Christian Ministry Resources
PO Box 1098
Matthews, NC 28106

(704) 841-8066
Fax (704) 841-8039

© Copyright 1997 by Charles Elliott
All rights reserved
ISBN 1-880562-29-4

Christian Ministry Resources

PO Box 1098, Matthews, NC 28106 (704) 841-8066, Fax (704) 841-8039

Erratum — page 5, paragraph 1: panning should be planning.

Contents

95290

Chapter 1

Approaches to Planning

One of the most pressing needs of the vast majority of congregations today is for help in strategic planning. Given seventeen "priority areas" to choose from, nearly half a nationwide sample of pastors, treasurers and church secretaries named strategic panning as their first or second priority. No other activity scored nearly as high. My guess is the felt need for help in devising ways to envision and plan for a future is not confined to the pastoral ministry. It is, I believe, shared by many people who are responsible for the church's outreach programs: from schools and hospitals to inner city programs, adult literacy or social housing.

It is not hard to see why. We are a pilgrim people or we are nothing. We proclaim a God who calls his people forward, as he called Abraham out of Ur of Chaldees; as he called Israel out of Egypt; and the Babylonian exiles back to Jerusalem. We are a people on the move. We carry no scrip or staff. We pray for our daily bread. We travel light because we expect to travel far. So we are a restless people, a people called to be on the move, knowing that we have here no continuing city, no solid certainties of routine or regularity, no comfortable sitting tight in the ample bosom of the status quo. If we are at ease in Zion, we are missing the point. Ours is a long, hard journey. If we settle too soon or too long, we have lost our flavor and are good only for the waste disposal unit.

That is common ground. Where it becomes more difficult is translating this sense of being called forward, or *out* as the Bible often has it, into practical action. The overall vocation to be on the move is easily understood in general: it is much harder to put it into practice.

The reasons for that are easy to find. First, we are quickly aware of the range and scale of demands on the church, and the relative paucity of resources. The homeless need shelter. The poor need food. The lonely need companionship. The sick need visiting. The bereaved need a chance to talk about their loved one. And that's just the very obvious, self-presenting outreach needs. Then the fabric of the church needs refurbishment. The music needs improving. The youth program is ready for an overhaul. The discipleship training of the young adults needs developing. And we have not started thinking about evangelizing the unchurched, addressing major policy issues in the locality, state or nation that are of vital concern to Christians or raising our gaze from our own ecclesiastical navels to the church overseas in any of its many guises. We may be a people called to be on the move, but where in this welter of need and opportunity are we supposed to move to?

The second reason why we find it hard to translate the general vocation to be a pilgrim people into reality is that we are often unsure whose job it is to make it happen. Is it the minister's? Or the lay leader's? Does it belong to the whole church? I shall have much more to say about this later in this chapter; for the moment I just want to flag the fact that the strategic planning of our mission as a pilgrim people often gets stuck because we are uncertain whose role it is to carry out that planning.

And that raises the third reason. Because we are often unsure about the "who" questions, and because we are nearly always unsure about the "what" questions, we too often get locked into arguments about both. Arguments lead to conflicts. Conflicts threaten to divide and even destroy the congregation, so the issues that generate them are best avoided. That's the end of strategic planning. We go back to a safe "maintenance ministry" well within everyone's comfort zone, and thereby begin the slow but certain suffocation of the life of the Church. We know with our heads that a church that is not seeking to live out the gospel in all aspects of its life has already within it the seeds of its own death, but in our hearts we want to avoid the conflict that planning for that living- out might bring.

If these reasons ring bells with your own experience, do not despair. I shall be suggesting that there are ways through; that we can find methods that are fun, inclusive and enriching, that minimize conflict, and which enable us to move joyfully but professionally into a proper engagement with our vocation as the people of God. But before I get to that, I want to paint another scenario which may also sound familiar. It is a scenario concerned not with the reasons why we are so reluctant to start strategic planning for our church or congregation, but rather why we often do it badly or in a way that fails to enrich the life of the whole congregation. Many ministers and even many church officers are anxious to make their mark; to show how efficient, dynamic, professionally competent and caring they are. By saying that I am not calling into question their motivation; many are motivated by a genuine love of Christ and compassion for his people. What I am calling into question is their sense of strategy. I often find church leaders are so anxious to do something that they do not find time to think carefully about priorities, about resources, about sequencing or sustainability.

A young minister here was appalled by the number of homeless people on our streets and, full of compassion for them, set about persuading the Elders of his church to convert the basement into a night shelter. Money was raised; the conversion carried out; the shelter opened. Within a year, the church found that they had not the resources, human or financial, to maintain the night shelter at a level minimally required by the authorities. Despite heroic endeavors, sacrificial giving of time and money, and desperate appeals to fellow Christians in the area for help, the church was obliged to allow the fire and hygiene authorities to issue a closure order. The homeless are back on the street; the church is in debt; and a number of faithful Christians are bruised and saddened.

I tell this story not to blame the minister or his church: they were doing what they could to meet an urgent need in the community in the name of Christ. In some ways they achieved more than they ever thought they could. The bottom line, however, was that they had not judged aright either the scale of the need or the resources at their disposal in the longer term, nor, for that matter, the impact of this one program on the life of the church and the community as a whole. Perhaps it is stories like these, repeated thousands of times, that explain the survey findings with which I started this chapter: the widespread felt-need for help in strategic planning.

So how do we go about it? We do not find it easy. We may easily get it wrong or, like the church I've just described, go off at half-cock. How do we do it?

Let's start by reviewing two ways that are currently in use. You may want to reflect which of these sketches best describes your own experience.

Leadership from the front

The first is what you might call leadership from the front. The minister or some other charismatic figure in the congregation produces a "vision" of what the church should be or become. That vision is then "sold" to the lay leadership who are expected to "buy into it." (These commercial terms are revealing.) The charisma of the minister can sustain the process for a time, usually at a high personal cost, both spiritually and emotionally. Then comes burn out. The minister breaks, experiences despair, and fights with the lay leadership. The vision disappears in a puff of acrimony.

Now you may think that portrait is over-drawn, and of course, as a representation of every example of charismatic leadership, it is. For I acknowledge that much fine work has been done by people operating within that style of leadership. Nonetheless, we need to be aware of the tendencies that can cause difficulties for this style of strategic planning. They boil down to unsustainability because this style depends too centrally on the energy of one person. And that remains true no matter how well the vision is "sold" or how whole heartedly others "buy into" it. Since it is a seller/buyer relationship, rather than a shared commitment, a genuinely collaborative discernment, it brings huge emotional and organizational costs that are too apt to spiral out of control.

The traditional model

At the other end of the spectrum of organizational styles is one that has been imported from the business world. It begins with mapping needs and resources and looking at the fit between them. It prioritizes needs according to a set of criteria: *immediate, urgent; important but not urgent, mainstream, secondary,* and then distributes resources to the meeting of those needs.

Now there is nothing intrinsically wrong with that style of strategic thinking: there are, however, a number of significant reservations one might have about its use in the average congregation. First, it is essentially technocratic. It depends on quite a high level of expertise in identifying resources, prioritizing needs, and matching one to the other. Any one can do this—*badly.* It takes quite rare skills to do it well, in a way that will be sustainable and mutually reinforcing. It is a rare congregation that has in-house the necessary expertise to go this route.

Even if, however, we assume that there are people in the congregation who have a high level of skills in this area (and it is not just the minister pretending to have such skills), where does that leave everyone else? On the outside, feeling manipulated by a priesthood of experts who will deliver a "Plan" to be accepted or rejected by the church at large.

That is the second reservation. The traditional form of strategic planning goes little way to honor the contribution that everyone can make to thinking through the future of their church. Sure there can be a consultation exercise. Sure the planning can be "open." Sure people can be given the chance to say what they think. Nonetheless, the central processes of collecting and analyzing the data tend to be non-participatory. Too often I have seen the results: an *in-group* who are excited and committed, and an *out-group* who feel manipulated, alienated, hurt and angry. The former get frustrated with the latter, whom they charge with not pulling their weight: the latter feel either that they are being taken for granted or, worse, that the in-group has somehow "taken our church from us," as one lady put it to me. In either case, the church has been weakened rather than strengthened, no matter how technically excellent the "plan" may be.

The third reservation is a little different, and begins to take us nearer the heart of what this book is about. Traditional strategic planning begins by identifying needs or problems. The church roof needs fixing. The youth group needs new premises. The minister's office needs bringing up to date. The organ needs overhauling. The outreach program needs a total redesign and so on. On one such exercise that I was involved in not long ago, the leadership of the congregation had no difficulty in identifying no less than thirty-one "needs" which they regarded as immediate or urgent! As they surveyed the list, hanging forbiddingly on lengths of shelf paper on the wall, I asked them how they felt. There was a long silence. Eventually one middle aged business man muttered, "Miserable." There was a murmur of agreement. "Near despair," someone else said. "It's impossible," came another voice.

That is not the mood out of which exciting and sustainable plans are made. Indeed you need to be both a sadist and a masochist to put people into a psychological position where all they can see are the deficits, the deficiencies, the problems, the needs, the gaps, the failures. Even if you start with the resources they have at their command, the negative psychological strength of the problems always seems stronger: and my experience in church planning is that the needs always far outweigh the resources anyway. (And in a way, so they should. If the church exists for those outside it, their needs are always likely to swamp the resources of those inside it.) Yet think of what that is doing to the people whose commitment, enthusiasm and dedication are fundamental to putting the plan into action. Psychically it is destroying them. And that means that, at the very least, it is in danger of destroying their spirit, their own human essence, made in the likeness of God. It is hard to think of anything more deeply in conflict with the primary task of the Church.

Now this suggests that we need to rethink our whole approach to strategic planning. We need to involve everyone, so that no one thinks they are not being taken seriously or their gifts are being ignored. And we need to reaffirm their life as a church, as a pilgrim people, by acknowledging their achievements, their gifts, their faithfulness. And finally we need to shift the focus from an oppressive sense of "the problems" to a joyful recognition of the goodness and glory of God: a goodness and glory that is waiting to reveal itself in the ordinary stuff of the everyday life of the congregation.

In the next chapter I shall argue that *appreciative inquiry* allows us to meet all these criteria. It offers us a way into strategic planning for the congregation that draws on the strengths of the whole congregation; that affirms and encourages them; but which challenges them to stretch themselves beyond what they thought was possible, without the risk of breaking them with a sense of the impossibility of the task or the inadequacy of their resources.

Chapter 2

Appreciative Inquiry

In this chapter, I shall first give you a better idea of what appreciative inquiry is all about. This will be a very introductory treatment, but one that enables me to say something, secondly, about its relationship with the faith and practice of the Church. I believe that the methods we use for planning and implementing our common life as the people of God have to reflect something of what we believe about the God we proclaim and about the kind of life He calls us to live. Unless there is that inner coherence and consistency, we soon lay ourselves open to the charge of hypocrisy and undermine the witness we seek to live. Having thus explored the compatibility of the appreciative approach with what we are all about, I can, in the next chapter, begin a more detailed "how to do it" account of the nuts and bolts of appreciative inquiry in action.

The best way of introducing appreciative inquiry is to invite you to reflect on two images. The first is a two pint jug containing one pint of milk. Is it half-full or half-empty? Either description is formally correct, but one focuses attention on what is there and the other focuses attention on what is missing. One creates an optimistic expectation: it is half-full and may one day be even fuller. The other creates a pessimistic expectation: it is half-empty and is draining away. Stretching the point just a little, we could say one focuses on what has been achieved—the jug has been filled; while the other focuses on what has been lost—the "missing" half.

The other image is a little more complex but can be introduced with a silly story. Two frogs fell into the jug of milk we imaged in the last paragraph. One was a very intelligent, analytically-bright, strategic-thinking frog. He calculated angles, measured heights, compared trajectories, and jumped. His calculations may have been right, but his muscles were not up to the job. Time and again he jumped, but he never made it to the rim. Exhausted he fell back into the milk and drowned. The other frog was a more reflective, appreciatively-inclined frog. He got to thinking about what capacities he had that would make a difference to his situation. Eventually he remembered that he had two powerful, webbed feet. With these he stirred the milk until it turned to butter. Standing on the butter he leapt out of the jug.

The appreciative approach, then, starts with a positive construction of the world. There is a good reason for this. It stems from the belief that we have an element of choice about how we see the world. The finer philosophical points that lie behind this belief need not detain us here: for our purposes we need only grasp that it is up to us whether we "see" a glass half-full or half-empty. There is no "right" or "true" answer: it is all in the eye of the beholder. In the same way as we look at the life of our congregation, we can, to a degree, choose how we see it. We can see it as full of defects, deficiencies, failures and set-backs; or we can see it as having sometimes, perhaps only very occasionally, been full of the love and light of the Holy Spirit. If we frame our questions aright (which we will explore in later chapters), we shall learn that for most of our people there are peak moments in their lives as Christians when "it all makes sense," "it all comes together," "we glimpse something of what the church is about." Appreciative inquiry starts (but does not end) with those moments of truth, insight and beauty, drawn from the experience of the whole people of God.

And then to return to the frogs: appreciative inquiry focuses on what people have, not on what they lack. It asks us to discover in each other the resources we have overlooked; the triumphs, however small and insignificant, that we can claim; the moments when we have uncovered for ourselves the goodness of God at work in His world.

As we shall see, this is not to deny the negatives, but it is to reframe them in a context which recognizes that we are in touch with a loving God who wills only the best for his people. It is to recognize that God the Creator *saw that it was good,* however marred, ruined and distorted it might subsequently have become. Or, to put it another way, appreciative inquiry does not deny the fact of sin, but it does insist that Christ offers us a way beyond our sins. It is the risen and glorified Christ that has the last word, not the fact of human sinfulness. We can choose which we see as primary: the failure and ugliness of sin, or the glory of the creator God. When we operate in the appreciative mode, we recognize the primacy of the goodness of God, but that does not prevent us from acknowledging all the horrors of human shortcoming. Reframed in the story of the birth, death and resurrection of Jesus Christ, however, they need not hold the same power or the same deadly destructiveness on what it means for us to be the church. That might sound all very well in theory; we shall see later that it is critically important in practice.

Appreciative inquiry, then, encourages and enable us to see beyond the smudginess of our own shortcomings to where God is at work, revealing himself in the workaday life of our community. And it does that by putting us in touch with the peak experiences of all the people of God in that community. There are two points here and I want to treat them separately. The first is that the method depends upon casting the net as wide as possible. Everyone is included in. I never cease to be moved and delighted by the way the appreciative method gives voice to people who have been ignored or acknowledged only formally for nearly all their lives. I think of a janitor who stood up before a crowded meeting and started by saying, "No one has ever asked my opinion before." He then went on to give a lucid and profound account of what he valued in the church where he was employed. Or I recall a "little old lady" (see how the stereotypes

14

stick!) who expressed delight that "even though I shan't live long enough to see all this come about, I feel part of you all now in a way I haven't for the last twenty years. And that's a good note to go out on."

But let's be clear about this. Why I think the inclusivity of the method is important is not some fad of political correctness. Nor is it because the more inclusive the method, the more energy will be released in the community as a whole. (Though that is not unimportant.) Why I think it is biblically significant is because it is a wonderful way of acknowledging the "priesthood of all believers." This deeply Pauline conviction, constantly repeated by the great Reformers, that every baptized Christian who is in communion with his or her church has a responsibility for the whole body of Christ, is too easily lost to sight in our high-pressured, specialized ministries where professionalism of performance is allowed to dominate the less glamorous gifts of the mass of the people.

Yet our experience, and that of anyone active in ministry who makes time to listen carefully, is that God deals faithfully with all his people. Sure, he gives different gifts and calls to different vocations. That is exactly why for St. Paul the body imagery is so fitting. A corollary of that imagery, however, is that every organ has a role to play. It may be humble or it may be exalted. It may be highly visible or it may be quite invisible. But the body as a whole ignores or demeans even the most humble, invisible organ at its own great peril. Consider the spleen or the sphincter.

You will immediately see the contrast with the charismatic and rationalist approaches to strategic planning we considered in the last chapter. They are technocratic or highly concentrated in one person. The appreciative method casts the net wide and includes everyone in. It starts from the assumption that everyone has something to contribute and that everyone's story is worth listening to because God is at work in the lives of every one of us.

That raises the second issue. As we shall see, the appreciative method proceeds by collecting the peak experiences of all the "stakeholders" in the church. That means that it plugs into the memories of God's dealing with the people; and with their responses to that dealing. It is not fanciful, I believe, to draw a straight parallel between that process and the writing of the Bible. The Bible is a collection of memories: of individuals; of communities; of schools of prophets; of, in the case of the New Testament, small, struggling groups of Christians, often in hostile environments. As they reflect on what has been happening to them as they try to approach God—on how God has been revealing himself in the history of their times—they create the traditions out of which the Bible comes to be written. They are, if you will, flesh becoming the word.

Now what I find so exhilarating about the appreciative method is that it is the same process relived in our own communities. We become the flesh that makes the word: the word of how God is at work in our midst and therefore how we can better respond to that Presence among us. By collecting each other's stories, by tapping into the memories that we share and the memories that may be unique to one of us, we, as it were, build up our own witness to where God has been leading us, and therefore where we need to follow in the future. And because we are looking for the work of God among us, it is an impossible arrogance to suggest that he has favorites or that he limits himself to some priestly or executive caste. If you are serious about trying to catch hold of God, you had better cast the net as wide as you dare.

Let me take this thought a step further. One way of thinking about the church is to think of it as a *library of memories*. Its foundational document is the Bible, proclaiming God's word through the memories of Abraham, Moses, the prophets, Paul, John of Patmos and others. But the church also functions to keep alive the memory of the great saints, the biblical saints and the saints of history, from St. Augustine to the "saints" of our own day, say Mother Teresa. What all these memories have in common is that they tell us something about God and the way he is at work bringing healing and salvation to his people. It is those memories that hold the church together: that give it continuity and a sense of its own identity. By tapping into our memories of God, we are adding our mite to the store of material we have, and are therefore putting our stamp on the identity of the church in our own day. In this sense, the appreciative method is not just about strategic planning as a management tool: it is about learning to be the church, and about learning who we are as the church.

Appreciative inquiry does not only draw on our memories, both individual and collective. It also draws on our imaginations. It draws us into a process whereby we envision a future. I regard this as potentially a deeply spiritual and Spirit-filled process. Certainly the biblical record is clear that envisionment is a gift of the Spirit. Abraham, Jacob, Isaiah, Ezekiel, Peter and John of Patmos, to mention only a few of the biblical examples, are all represented as being given as a gift of God the ability to see beyond the pall of the present to a deeper reality. As we go through the appreciative method to plan strategically for the future of our church or congregation, we are not just using our intellectual capacities, in the way a salesman might project his sales figures forward for five years, but we are seeking to discern the will of God for our little corner of his Body. And the way we do that is to invite him, through the Person of the Holy Spirit, to use the imaginative powers we have been given, as we reflect on what we have learned from each other of the way he has been working among us in the past.

Naturally different Christian traditions have different disciplines for this prayerful process of discernment. Some, such as the Roman Catholics, have carefully worked out approaches, like the Ignatian Exercises, tried and tested over the centuries. Others have less formalized styles; and others still, coming from the Pentecostal tradition, have their own ways of responding to the Spirit. I am less concerned with the methods of prayer and discernment that are used in this context: what I am concerned to establish is that the "envisioning" part of the appreciative method is seen as an essentially

God-centered one, dependent upon the work of the Spirit among his people. It is a creative act, and like all acts of creation, it depends finally upon the one great Creator.

This comes the more naturally and spontaneously if the prior work of listening empathetically to the stories of God's dealing with his people has been accorded the time and patience it needs. For it is in the interpenetration of the memories of the past and the yearning for the future that the Spirit can mobilize our imaginations, delivering us simultaneously from *illusions* about what we are and from *fear* of what we might become. Those are the two major spiritual threats to this process; I need to say a word about each.

Illusion

There is a strong revelatory function to envisionment, as even a cursory reading of the Old Testament and, even more, of the Revelation of St. John will bring out. What is revealed is the reality of the present situation, shorn of its comforting simplicities and its easy compromises. "The truth will make you free," and it does so by removing all the buttresses of our self-regard and self-satisfaction. One of the dangers of our memory work is that we remember what is comfortable to remember: indeed there is plenty of evidence in the social psychology literature that our mind "shapes and fits" what we remember and how we remember it. In that sense our memories may be biased towards the "self" with which we are most comfortable, even though that construction of the self is, in some ways, seriously deficient. We need, then, a power beyond ourselves, not to unmake those memories, but rather to ensure that we do not too easily accept them as the final definition of either the present, or, even more important, of the future.

Fear

Again and again, both Old and New Testaments warn us against fear. From Moses to Mary to "the little flock," the people of God are told not to fear the future, but to trust the gracious purposes and promises of God. Fear and trust are the mirror images of each other. Fear destroys; trust liberates. Fear condemns to the present; trust opens the rich possibilities of the future. Fear makes real vision impossible, just as it makes real love impossible. Yet as we plan for the future of the Body of Christ, in whatever local representation we are concerned with, love has to be the essence of what we are about. That realization takes us to the heart of the prayerfulness that under-girds the use of our imaginations in envisioning the future. For we need to be in touch with the very ground of our love, the deepest springs of what gives meaning and coherence to our lives if we are to surrender ourselves to the leading of the Spirit as we search for God's future. And that "being in touch" is ultimately grace. It is gift. It is not something we can win for ourselves by effort or cleverness or technique or moral worth. We have to trust that this loving Father-God we proclaim will honor his promises to his people.

That is a good place to draw this initial discussion of the spiritual dimension of the appreciative approach to an end—with the loving promises of God. For that is the final reality. Beside it the details of the appreciative method; the do's and don'ts; the record of how it has worked in practice count for nothing. It is well to remember what a terrible thing it is to fall into the hands of the living God: a terror made tolerable by gut-knowledge of the infinite compassion of God. For when appreciative inquiry works at its best, we are indeed surrendering ourselves into the hands of the living God.

That does not imply, however, that we release all responsibility for the process. Far from it. In the next chapter we shall take a closer look at what that process involves.

Chapter 3

Foundational Elements

In chapter 1 I explored the advantages that the appreciative method offers any church or congregation that is seeking to plan its way forward strategically. In the last chapter I looked at some of the spiritual dimensions of the process, emphasizing the interpenetration of prayer, in its broadest sense, and appreciative inquiry. In this chapter I shall take the reader step by step through the various elements of an appreciative inquiry; and in the chapters 4-8 we will eavesdrop on a congregation as it uses the method for its own purposes.

So let's begin at the beginning.

Step 1. Deciding

A church decides (we can leave on one side for the moment the question of how it may have reached that decision) that it needs a strategic plan for the next five years, and is wondering how to do it. We saw some of the options in chapter 1 (there are of course many others) and no doubt some members will want to use one method and others another. That is normal and, within limits, perfectly healthy. Perhaps one option that will be discussed in this context is appreciative inquiry. Now it is my experience that the inquiry will be much easier to manage and will generate much more energy if the church as a whole makes a conscious, well informed and properly debated decision to go down this track.

The first step, then, in any appreciative inquiry is to explain the basic elements to as many people as are willing to listen; to invite their participation and to encourage them to feel that they "own" what they are committing themselves to. We shall look at various ways this might be done in chapters 4 and 8: for the moment I want to emphasize only that the skill and sensitivity with which this initial step is taken will heavily influence the "feel" of the rest of the process.

Step 2. Choosing the Work Group

Once agreement has been reached that the strategic plan is to be developed using appreciative inquiry, the next step is the formation of what is usually known as a "work-group" to oversee the process. This needs to honor the participative and collaborative style of the appreciative method: it calls for something more than the minister and the church officers. We will come back to how the work group might be chosen: I need to emphasize here the importance of it being recognized throughout the church or congregation that it is in some sense representative; that it is inclusive; and that it sees itself as accountable to the whole church community.

It is not easy to be precise about how big the work group needs to be. There are good theoretical reasons for preferring a number between seven and ten, but I have known both larger and smaller work groups function triumphantly well. What is important is that whoever is on the work group is committed to attending all, or very nearly all, the meetings. Birds of passage should be avoided. Potential members of the work group need to be assured that it is riveting and sometimes even thrilling work: but it is demanding of time, energy and commitment.

Step 3. Forming the questions

Once the work group has been selected and has shaken down together (we will look at ways that can be achieved in chapter 4), it can begin the work. The first task of the work group is the development of what is known in the trade as "an appreciative protocol." If that sounds intimidating, don't let it be: it is actually perfectly simple. An appreciative protocol is no more than a list of "guiding questions" that people can use to help steer them through the collection of memories and stories to which I referred in the last chapter.

There is, however, a certain art in framing these guiding questions. I will have more to say about this in chapters 4 and 9, but for the moment we need to be clear about two things. First, the tone of the questions, as well as their substance and direction, will determine the way the inquiry develops. Second, and related to that, the questions are designed to elicit stories about when the congregation or church was at its best: when did people feel most inspired; most in touch with the goodness and graciousness of God; closest to the Kingdom of God. The questions are generative in this sense: they are a search for what has, in the past, given energy, meaning and inspiration to the people. As we shall see, that is not to allow the past to set bounds to the future: but it is to encourage people to reflect on the history of God's dealing with this congregation and discover where he has been leading them.

So what might an appreciative protocol look like? We shall return to this, but here are two examples:

Appreciative protocol 1.

Tell me a story about when St. Mark's was most alive for you.

What do you most value about St. Mark's?

Tell me what has happened in the life of St. Mark's that you think creates the greatest joy in heaven?

What do you think are St. Mark's richest blessings?

What do you think is God's dearest wish for how St. Mark's should be in five years time?

Appreciative protocol 2.

When are you most pleased that you are a member of this congregation?

Taking the congregation as a whole, when do you think we are most joyful, energized and most effective as Christians? Tell me some stories about it.

What excites you personally about this congregation?

If Jesus walked in today, what do you think would give him most pleasure about our life together as a congregation? If he walked in five years time, what changes would give him the greatest pleasure?

You will notice that there is much in common between these two protocols. Perhaps the greatest difference is only in the wording. Each is trying to enable every member of the group to get in touch with the features of their common life that are most inspiring, most creative, most energizing, most consonant with the life of Christ.

It is important to emphasize, however, that these are not mechanical questions on some questionnaire, which can be read off like a supermarket marketing survey and ticked off as "done." They are guides to the kind of conversation that will generate the most helpful stories, the most reflective and even profound recollections of the peak experiences of the life of the group. It is those stories that will tell us where the real energy in the congregation is: where they are, as a group, beginning to discover the dimensions of their vocation as a people of God.

Step 4. Asking the questions

Using these guiding questions, members of the work group hold "appreciative conversations" with every member of the church who is willing to take part. If the prework of consensus building round the appreciative approach has been done well, that will be the huge majority of members—so it is quite a task! In a large organization or church of a thousand members or more, it may well be beyond the grasp of the members of the work group to conduct all the conversations themselves. In that case, the process is cascaded down so that the first, say, ten "interviewees" each ask another ten the same kinds of questions. With this multiplier effect of the cascade, even very large numbers can be handled without too much difficulty—provided proper training and support is given to all the "interviewers." (I put that word in quotes to remind us that it is a mistake to think of these conversations as interviews). If they get as formal and stereotyped as an interview, they are largely missing the point. And that is one reason why some training of each cadre of people who are going to apply the protocols, the "interviewers," is well worth while.

An important issue that has to be decided here is how many people outside the immediate "family" of the church should be included. In commercial applications of appreciative inquiry, we usually suggest that the inquiry be extended to (a sample of) all stakeholders: customers, suppliers, bankers and so on. This helps the organization gain a more rounded perspective on itself and can often lead to major shifts in the later parts of the process. In the case of a church school or hospital, the similar identification of the stakeholders who might be included is unlikely to be too difficult. In the case of a church or congregation, more imagination might be necessary. Who are the people who know the church well, care much about it, but are not members and therefore might bring a fresh perspective?

There is no one answer to this question: in some situations you might think of involving people from a neighboring church, from different denominations, from different "levels" in the church hierarchy. Perhaps even more important but probably harder to bring off is to involve people in the local community, especially significant figures in the community like a doctor, a school teacher, the town mayor, perhaps even the editor of the local paper or TV station. They may not be able to answer all the questions in the protocol: but they will be able to tell stories about the "best" of the church from their perspective, and they may have their own dreams for its future.

Step 5. Identifying the themes

Once the conversations have been carried out, the stories that emerge are the precious data of the inquiry. They will need to be sifted, sorted and put into categories. The data themselves will define the most helpful categories, but a fairly typical approach would be to divide them into those that relate to (a) the worshipping life of the church; (b) the teaching/training life of the church; (c) the outreach programs (which may need much further subdivision); (d) the caring and fellowship dimensions of the church, and (e) administration, finance and personnel. A more creative way to do it would be to collect the stories from different elements of the congregation: the senior citizens, the young parents, the teenagers and so on and see what themes emerge from each age group.

However the data are dissected, the core remains the stories. They need to be told and retold, shared over as wide a group as possible so that everyone can hear (or read) what has been life-giving and life-changing for their fellow Christians. Usually this business of sharing the stories is one of the most exciting and eye- opening stages in the process. People are presented with the most profound, even most holy, moments of their fellow worshippers: the effect is often deeply moving. As one elderly and very conservative gentleman put it to me: "I had no idea. It's astonishing. We were looking for God outside and he was here among us all the time. We shall never be the same again."

Step 6. Forming the Future

This step is in some ways the most important, and perhaps the most demanding. People enjoy telling stories about the past, doing the memory work. Now they are going to do the imaginative work, and many of us find that challenging and unsettling. It is therefore important, I believe, to put this firmly into the context of liturgy, of the deliberate coming-into-the-Presence of God. We can hold over for a later chapter suggestions about how that may be done; now we need to get at the heart of what is going on at the group-process level.

In the jargon of the trade, the work group is about to form "provocative propositions." These are vision statements, which take as their starting point the "best" of the experiences described in the stories, but stretches that "best" to just, but only just, beyond the present reach of the group. The statements are couched in the present tense, as if they describe reality as it currently is. Provocative propositions that have come out of recent work with congregations include the following.

This church offers unconditional love to all needy people in our community, wherever and whenever they can receive it.

We create the worshipping environment in which each person, irrespective of denominational allegiance, gender, age or status, can experience for themselves the presence and compassion of God.

As a community we live the life of the Beatitudes and are blessed accordingly.

We honor our young people as the channels of God's grace to their generation, and we express that honor by according them a full role in the governance of the church.

Meadowbrook is an open church: open to whomsoever needs to be here for whatever reason.

I smile as I write these provocative propositions, because the aspirations they express are far removed from the present reality that I, as a visitor with a trained eye, could observe. To take the last example. Meadowbrook (not its real name) was actually a rather stuffy, wealthy, middle class church whose abiding sin was self-indulgence. The point was that the process had allowed its people to see that for themselves, and to have the courage to challenge themselves at their weakest point. For them to envision the time when Meadowbrook would be open to drunks, hoboes, prostitutes, homeless people and the mentally disturbed was an amazing act of grace.

It was both an act of deep discernment and simultaneously an act of shattering repentance. As the gentleman quoted above said, "We shall never be the same again."

Step 7. Sharing the dream

The provocative propositions will emerge from the work group that has been looking at the data and collecting feed back from the retelling of the stories. Before they can form the basis of the strategic plan, however, three things must happen. They must be endorsed by the whole group. They must be tested for practicality. And they must be tested (or retested) for their provocative quality. A word about each of these without getting hung up at this stage about the precise techniques that might be used for each of these sub-steps.

Building a consensus around the key provocative propositions is obviously essential. They have emerged from the stories of the group, but they have been hammered into shape, sometimes with considerable difficulty, by the work group. Now they need to be repossessed by the church or congregation as a whole. When they can consciously make an act of ownership, they can assume responsibility for translating present reality into the state described in the provocative proposition. We look at ways we have used to encourage this consensus and ownership in chapters 8 and 9.

Overly utopian provocative propositions are unhelpful at best and destructive at worst. "Pie in the sky" feeds no one. It is therefore often helpful to check the practicability of provocative propositions by asking people to rank the provocative propositions in order of doability. If there is near unanimity that one proposition is the least doable, it probably needs looking at again, and possibly dropping altogether. Again, I shall suggest the nuts and bolts of how this can be done in chapter 9.

Step 8. Planning for Action

Once you have a set of just-do-able provocative propositions "owned" by the whole congregation, you can move into action planning. I want to make only three points about this.

The first is that the stories, which formed the core of the data from which the provocative propositions have been drawn, will almost certainly contain material that helps identify the people and resources available for action. Sometimes it is helpful to include a question in the protocol that is designed specifically to elicit this kind of information. Such a question might, for example, take the form: "What do you most enjoy doing in the life of the church?" Or "Without being unduly modest, what do you think you are best at doing in the life of the church?"

Even without such direct questions, however, we usually find that the stories that people tell about their best experiences of the life of the church are a rich source of information about what they, and their families, friends, neighbors and even their community, can bring to the life of the church. Indeed it is surprising how often the "peak experience" described is precisely an experience of being challenged and stretched to offer more than is conventionally demanded. (And that is true over a far wider canvas than money alone.)

Second, in the action planning it is vital to remain in appreciative mode; that is to say, the nature of the conversation should continue to refer to the experiences of the "best," the "most energizing," the "deepest." It is worth stressing this because we all tend to slip back into problem-dominated thinking or into analytical right/wrong type discussion when faced with the issue of what we are going to do and who is going to do it. As we shall see in a later chapter, the role of the facilitator here can be very important: it is his or her job to "hold" the group in the appreciative mode and that is best done by constantly taking them back to the stories.

Third, action planning is about action! That means that, while staying in the appreciative mode, the questions of *who, what, why, when,* and *accountable to whom* have to be asked and answered. If the stories have done their job and if the whole community has really heard those stories, this distribution of tasks does not feel like an imposition. It feels like a chance to recreate, hopefully on a permanent basis, what gives meaning, joy and fulfillment to the people charged with those tasks.

This change in the psychological or spiritual dynamics is one of the great gifts that appreciative method has to bring to the church. If we start by identifying a "problem" and then cast about for a "solution," the person(s) charged with implementing the solution are likely to feel that this is one more task that has to be done "to solve the problem." They may tackle it willingly and get some satisfaction from doing what has to be done, but they are likely to be doing it because they feel they "ought" to. A sense of obligation drives them. By contrast if they are moving out of the appreciative mode, they are doing something that they have identified as life-enriching. They are drawn to it by their own experience. It is this difference between being driven and being drawn which is central. It is akin to Baron von Hügel's aphorism: "Devils drive; God draws."

Now we have reviewed the basic steps in appreciative inquiry, we need to see it in action. The next chapters therefore present a congregational case study of an appreciative inquiry. It is fictional in the sense that, partly to disguise the locale and partly because I need the freedom to exhibit a range of factors, not all of which are likely to be present to the same degree in any one case, I have drawn upon the experience of a number of similar exercises. But the individual elements of the case study are factual and the whole is designed to give the reader a better understanding of what the approach "feels" like from the inside. This will pave the way for a more detailed discussion of the method in chapter 9.

Chapter 4

St. Luke's

St. Luke's is a church set on the fringes of a medium sized town not far from Cleveland, Ohio. Perhaps surprisingly, its congregation does not include many commuters: they tend to live on the other side of town. Most of the people in the church would fall into one of these three groups: retired or approaching retirement age; blue-collar workers, mostly working in the medium-sized engineering firms in the town; young marrieds living in a development of affordable houses at the edge of the community, and mostly working in town in a wide variety of non-professional jobs. A few African-Americans live near the church: only a tiny handful worship regularly at St. Luke's.

It is not a rich, wealthy or prestigious congregation. Nor is it especially "successful" in terms of church-growth. The annual number of new members, a measure by which the church judges itself, has been rising less fast than the population of the community. Proportionately, therefore, it may well be true that the church has lost ground.

St. Luke's is a slightly old fashioned traditional congregation. The Sunday morning service is at the heart of the church, and much effort goes into making it an aesthetically pleasing occasion, with a choir and small orchestra. There is, however, emphasis on lay participation. A number of congregational members assist with reading the Scripture and participating in the service. Some are even organized and trained as "lay ministers."

The previous pastor had put much stress on lay training, with the result that, as well as the lay ministers group, there are three other "classes" of trainees. The first, a Young Peoples' Forum for the 15-19 age group, is mostly teenagers who are entering the adult world of work, booze, drugs, and sex. The intention is to stiffen their discipleship and discourage the drift away from the church that occurs among many teenagers. There has in fact been a drift away from the Forum. At the time of the intervention, numbers were less than a dozen.

The second group of trainees is a sustained spirituality workshop in which various traditions of prayer are explored and practiced. The membership is predominantly female and elderly, but the class has grown over the last eighteen months and generates real enthusiasm: the minister, who leads it, clearly has considerable gifts in this area.

The last group of "trainees" are the "stewardship stewards." They are trained to engage the congregation, and a few well wishers who for one reason or another do not often attend church, in reflection on the use of time, talents and money. This is a hang-over from a major campaign, led by external consultants about six years ago, which was designed to raise enough money to pay off the large debt the church had acquired as the result of an over ambitious building program. The debt is now almost extinguished, but the stewards have found that the kind of conversation they can introduce with members of the church is valuable in a far wider sense than merely financial. Some of them have become family counselors in everything but name, and they therefore value the continuing training/supervising sessions, led by a professional woman from outside the church. Their numbers are, however, down to five: two of the five have signaled their wish to retire from the post.

In terms of outreach and mission, the church's current stance is modest. The primary need to pay off the debt is given as the reason. There is a "missions weekend" when one of the major mission boards is invited to make a presentation. In general this is poorly supported.

The only sustained outreach into the local community is a "Singles Families Camp," when about twenty single parents take their children camping for a week. About half of the campers are nonmembers of the church. Despite quite generous subsidies, it has become increasingly hard to recruit them and this enterprise is in danger of collapse.

I was approached by the pastor, Peter, whom I had known sometime ago in a quite different context, for help in "thinking through who we are and where we are going, and perhaps where we ought to be going," as he put it in his letter. He had been in the church eighteen months, and had just been joined by Sam, a young, sparky female associate, fresh out of seminary. It was while introducing her to the daily routine of the church that he had realized that neither he nor the lay leadership in the church board had much sense of direction. Until now he had been wholly absorbed in finding his way round the church and getting to know the people, and then had allowed himself to be sucked into the abyss of meeting their (unrealistic and dependent) expectations of him. The arrival of Sam two months ago had made him stop and take a harder look at himself and his ministry. Hence his letter to me.

I arranged to spend a long weekend at the church. During that time I assembled the background data presented above and met as many of the leading people as I could. I was left with three impressions. First, Peter had succeeded a much loved pastor who had been in the church for over twenty years. He had seen himself as first and foremost a shepherd to his flock. In many ways it had been a successful and even inspiring ministry, but it had left ingrained patterns of dependency and introversion that Peter would find it hard, and his church members, painful, to break.

Second, I could not help noticing a cleavage in the congregation between the more senior members, many of whom had known and loved the previous pastor throughout his twenty years; and the younger people from the new development, to whom he had seemed ancient, unimaginative and boring. If their perspectives on the old pastor were worlds apart, so were their hopes and aspirations for the future. That is not to imply that the seniors were wholly stuck in the past: more perhaps that they were suspicious of a different future and not a little afraid of it. For them a "good pastor" was one who visited frequently, knew them and their families, remembered their birthdays and anniversaries, and could relieve their anxieties about this world and the next. They dreaded losing that type of ministry, while recognizing that the church needed a new kind of leadership if it was to grow in numbers and commitment.

Many of the younger people, mostly in their late twenties and thirties, and not as numerous or as vocal as the seniors, were sticking with the church despite the ghosts of the past in the hope that Peter, whom they liked and admired, could breathe new life into the place. They were understandably vague about what "new life" meant, but they were almost unanimous in their feeling that their age cohort was largely ignored in the present structures and activities. "Not that," added one of them with a rueful smile, "we have much spare capacity in terms of time. Life sometimes feels overfull already."

My third overwhelming impression was a lack of engagement with the real world. The service was fine in its detached way, but I wondered how easy people found it to relate to the rest of their lives. Famine in Africa was unfolding on our TV screens. It was ignored. One of the biggest local employers had gone under, with major job losses. No mention. Peter himself, once so broad and alert to his environment, seemed to have been drawn into this mind-set. He preached a scholarly sermon on the Incarnation; but failed to tell his people what difference it made to their lives. I found myself ruefully remembering Bishop Gore's dictum: "The deeper I get into the mystery of the Incarnation, the more interested I become in drains." I did not detect a similar interest in the real world in Peter's congregation.

I shared these three impressions with Peter and Sam when we met for a wrap-up session. Peter looked glum. "So where do we go from here?" he asked. "I know our problems and I acknowledge my own failings. What I don't seem to be able to get my head round is how to move us all forward. If we don't move, I know we are finished. Death by a couple of hundred coffins."

I was delighted that he did not have a private agenda that he was seeking to impose on his people while pretending to be "open." His confusion and sense of being lost I saw as a great strength. I asked if he had shared his feelings with any of the lay leadership. "Good grief, no!" he replied. "They think I have all the answers. That's why they appointed me. I can't go along to them and say, 'Sorry guys: I'm as clueless as the rest of you.' They'd be on the phone to church officials before you could turn round."

"I think you have two possible ways to go," I told Sam and Peter. "You can go with a technique like Future Search, which will get your people looking where they are and where they might go in response to the world around them. They will find that quite hard, I suspect, but it will help them change gear, see the life of the church and their own lives as faithful Christians in a quite different perspective. Or you can try appreciative inquiry, which you, Peter, know a little about already. The advantage of that is that it will draw in all your people, perhaps in a more engaging way than Future Search. The disadvantage is that no one can tell you where you will come out, and you will have no control of that. Maybe the fact that you have no control and will be seen by everyone to have lost control is exactly the reason for going with it. It will scare the daylights out of some of your people, maybe especially the seniors; but it will be a terror that will enable them to grow. Don't make a choice now. You have a lot of work to do getting your people ready for any kind of intervention and then enabling them to choose. That's crucial. They must not do it just because 'the pastor says so.' They need to be very intentional about it. And I suspect you are going to have to do a lot of prework to get them there."

We mapped out a plan for the prework, which would culminate in a half day conference on a Sunday in Lent. This prework had three elements. The first was a "social mapping" exercise. Derived from Robert Chambers' ideas about "participative rural appraisal," this involves the production of a large scale map of the community, on which are plotted all the member-families, with connections between them (blood, good friends, school companions, work mates) indicated by cotton threads of different colors. In the same way, the major nonchurch features of the community are highlighted on the map: community facilities like schools, hospitals, prisons, shopping malls, major employers, civic government offices and departments, and leisure facilities. More cotton threads link each family to the three locations they regard as the most important to them. (A variant is to have a fourth thread linking each family to the location in which they expect to see other members of the congregation.)

The value of this exercise is three fold. First it gets everyone involved. Second it reveals relationships among the congregation, and therefore reveals who are at the center of significant networks and who are relatively isolated. And third, it begins to get church members to see, with their own eyes, the ways in which they as a congregation relate to the wider world in the immediate vicinity. Although the information it reveals is hardly new or breath-taking, in my experience it always comes as a surprise and source of wonder to the people to see how many significant relationships there are between the member-families and the wider community.

The second element of the prework was no less simple, and no less revealing to the congregation. Each member-family was to select another to which the social map showed they were in no way linked, and ideally one spatially at a distance from them too. They were to ask that family—as a family—round for simple refreshment (not a banquet) and help the visitor family draw (not write) its history since it came to the congregation. The host family would then take the picture to church one Sunday, pin it up and, in the coffee hour after the main service, tell the family's history.

The intention behind this exercise was two fold. First was to try to mix the various elements of the congregation on a social level and get them to interact in a non-threatening but self-disclosing way. Second was to familiarize the people with the idea of their own history. This would come to play such a key role in the future search or the appreciative inquiry or, most likely, any other process they were to undertake, that it was worth taking some trouble at this initial stage to introduce it.

The third element of the prework was to introduce the idea of waiting on the Lord for the gift of vision into the praying life of the congregation. I suggested that this be done gradually, almost organically; and that it be allowed to grow naturally out of the spirituality workshops. I was keen to avoid using prayer as a bludgeon with which to beat the church into submission, or even the remotest possibility that it could be so interpreted. I hoped that, out of the prayer itself, a few people in the workshops would begin to want to share the yearning for a giant step forward. In my judgment, that yearning would arise spontaneously out of disciplined prayer in the group and would be uncontainable.

Sam and Peter set about implementing these three stages of the prework, taking care to discuss each as widely as they could, especially among those families that they felt were only loosely attached to St. Luke's. I suspect they were expecting some opposition from the church board: instead they received something much worse— almost total apathy. "They go along with it," Peter complained in one of our many long phone conversations: "but I think they would go along with topless dancers in the Sanctuary or three-hour prayer meetings at every service. I sometimes wonder if they switch off as soon as they enter the room." To me it seemed like further evidence that the dependency syndrome went deeper than I had imagined.

The processes did, however, begin to work their magic. By the time the social map was finished, Peter's telephoned reports were sounding much more upbeat, and he himself was beginning to shift emotionally from despondency to enthusiasm. "There's a real buzz round that map," he told me. "It's less what it reveals, though that has opened a lot of eyes, than the process. People get a lot of fun from seeing how they all relate to each other and where they go in town. For the first time, I get the sense that they are beginning to see themselves as something more than a bunch of isolated families who just happen to come to St. Luke's. And that's progress."

I was confident that the event that was to mark the end of the prework and pave the way for the design of the "real" intervention— the half day Conference of the whole church— would give this initial sense of movement a further push forward. With a little telephonic coaching from me, Sam and Peter and two of the leaders from the "Stewards" group designed a Wall of Wonder exercise as the central activity of the Conference. Like all good organizational-development exercises, this is in essence very simple. It is a visual history, with time expressed as a horizontal line. Years are marked off, starting as early as any one can remember and continuing to the present day. (In another variant, you can continue into the future, but we did not choose that option on this occasion.) The time-line is drawn in the middle of the paper, usually a series of sheets covering most of one wall. Then the group is asked to write into the appropriate year-columns what they remember as happening in that year. The exercise is given greater impact by the fact that they are also asked to record the event on a vertical line: the "better" the event, the higher up the sheet it is put. Disasters, tragedies, miseries thus sediment on the bottom; peak experiences occupy the high ground. At a glance you can see what the group has experienced as "good" and what it wants to forget.

Deciding

Passing over the details of how they ensured a high turn out and encouraged participation in "building" the Wall of Wonder, let me record Peter's account on the telephone that night.

"Incredible. Just incredible. I learned more about this place in three hours this morning than I have learned in eighteen months of dogged pastoring. I need time to digest it all, but all sorts of things are falling into place, and if that is true for Sam and me it must be even truer for a lot of our people. For example, I never knew that there had been a huge financial scandal, when the Treasurer was charged with embezzling $8,000. That was about ten years ago. No one ever mentions it. But it explains why many of the older folk are so uptight about the debt. They feel ashamed about it, as though they were personally responsible. That's ridiculous, I know. But it's clearly how they feel. But what touched me was the way some of the younger people reacted when the story came out. They were so sad for the older folks, comforting them, persuading them that it was OK, that the church is big enough to cope with that. That's an example from the downside. On the upside, Sam was struck, I don't know why I missed it: says plenty about me, huh? How little upside there was. Real upside. There are only two events in the last six years that were high on the sheet: the visit of Desmond Tutu in 1991 and the launch of the Stewardship campaign in 1990. Oh, yeah, and my appointment but someone had to say that, didn't they? I guess we are a mildly depressed congregation. So much for the glorious liberty of the children of light, eh? But oddly, that's not how it felt. People were not going around with faces as long as fiddles. There was a real buzz, a lot of laughter, banter, real enjoyment in that room. It's as if they have forgotten and/or don't want to remember the good things. Or did we somewhere make a hash of it?"

It was not hard to reassure Peter that he had not messed up. His experience is so typical that I could almost have written the script before his call. We are so unused to looking out for and valuing the "good" things that happen in our church life; and so fixated with the disasters, the conflicts, the failures and the petty irritations of the daily grind that the kind of response that Peter's wall of wonder had evoked is almost universal. Yet the cheerful buzz he reported shows that is not the whole truth. It is a half-truth we construct for ourselves and out of which we tend to operate: defensively, passively, cautiously, timidly. Clearly any major intervention that St. Luke's was going to undertake would have to challenge that construction, and emphasize its reverse.

We agreed that Peter and Sam would circulate to all members of St. Luke's a short introduction from me about both Future Search and Appreciative Inquiry. Every member would then be invited to an open forum which I would attend and at the end of that forum there would be a secret ballot with doing nothing as a third option. That would be regarded as an advisory opinion for further consideration by the church board. They would have the final decision, and thereby accept the final responsibility.

In the event and slightly to my surprise, the forum, gratifyingly well-attended, voted heavily in favor of an appreciative inquiry. That was endorsed somewhat less enthusiastically by the church board. Now we could begin.

Chapter 5

Getting Ready For Action

Choosing the work group

The first stage had to be the selection of a work group. The micro-politics were not unfamiliar, but were nonetheless tricky. The church board was formally responsible for the inquiry, but was dominated by seniors, many of whom were still emotionally in thrall to the former pastor. It did, however, contain some of the most highly trained of the lay leadership: the two most active Stewards were on the church board as were three of the lay ministers. Clearly lacking was adequate representation from the young marrieds and the late teenage groups. I suspected, and Sam confirmed, that there were also a few bright, able and willing people in the congregation who did not fall into any of these easy and targeted groups. I was especially aware of the four or five African-American families who were not exactly socially ostracized but who had difficulty inserting themselves into any of the existing patterns. I was sure in my own mind that their whole hearted participation would be a bonus worth playing for.

We needed to find a way of keeping the church board supportive, but simultaneously of incorporating under used talents and under-represented groups. Peter, Sam and I discussed many ways of achieving this while leaving the final decision to the church as a whole. If we were determined that the church board would not dominate the process, we were no less determined that we should not do so either. Peter was clear he would resist any attempt to "leave it to the pastor" now and at any future stage of the inquiry.

In the event we came up with a simple but effective strategy. We asked anyone who so wished to submit a "dream ticket" of five names for the work group with at least two names of people aged under 30. Peter excluded himself from nomination, but offered to act in an occasional consultancy role to the work group if invited. We received 65 lists, a number high enough to convince all of us that, however apathetic Peter found the church board, something was beginning to catch fire. Our prompting on including the younger members had worked and had spilled over to include the blacks. We ended up with Sam, the senior elder (also a lay minister), an unmarried mother of mixed blood who was a well known "character" (and also one of the most faithful attenders at the spirituality workshop), an African-American accounts clerk, and a college student who was the only talented soprano in the choir.

Peter was both puzzled and delighted. "It means many, many of the old folks have voted for more than the prescribed two youngsters. Now that is good news. In the past, they have seemed to me to want to pack the church board with their own. But on the work group we have only one person from the church board, and he's OK. He has great authority among the leaders, so if things get rough, he'll almost certainly keep the laggards on board."

I flew down for a weekend with the work-group to help them plan the whole inquiry and especially to frame the appreciative protocol and practice its use. It was clear that they would have to train a significant number of other members to administer it, so it was essential that they really understand what they were doing, both intellectually and emotionally.

After a few simple team-building exercises, they began to relax with each other, but I was aware that, short as time was, the success of the whole inquiry depended critically not just on how well they interacted with each other, but on how deeply they trusted each other. I therefore put them through an exercise of leading each other blindfolded through an obstacle course; and then round an electric barrier, seemingly plugged into a socket in the wall and therefore supposedly "live." This was followed by the elder leading us through a meditation on trust in God, based on St. John, chapter 14. He made the point that if we do not trust each other, we certainly will not trust God; and yet we were committing the future of St. Luke's to each other under God's providence. They got the point.

"We will grow into it," said the African American accounts clerk, a mite defensively. (Hardly surprising.)

"I'll tell you when you have reached a real trust in each other, and perhaps a real trust in God too," I replied, without in any way intending it as a challenge. "And that is when you can tell each other, in this open space, what you are most ashamed of."

Quite unplanned and wholly spontaneously, Sam spoke—very quietly and slowly. "I am ashamed of how jealous I have been and still am of my elder sister. I ask for deliverance from this jealousy every night, but it still consumes me. I cannot think of her without thinking of all she has—brains, looks, a great figure, a doctorate, a fantastic job, admirers by the truck load, and I seethe with hatred. And she goes on being sweet, kind, thoughtful, considerate to me. God, I hate myself for it." She shrunk into silence.

One by one they all spoke, making me check that they were really comfortable to do so. Finally it was my turn. It was not easy, but the sense of being bonded thereafter was something I shall never forget. I would unhesitatingly trust my life to that group, even now, some years later. And I know they feel the same. We had more to thank Sam for than she will ever know. I had now no doubts that this group would work together like silk on silk.

Forming the questions

On the second day, then, we were able to get down to drafting the appreciative protocol. First, I got the members of the work group to interview each other using three simple generative questions that I gave them. These were:

What makes you glad you are a member of St. Luke's? Tell me a story about it.

What do you think are the hidden strengths of St. Luke's?

What would you have liked to add to the top half of the wall of wonder?

I deliberately chose questions that were just off center for the purpose of this inquiry because it was important that the work group find its own questions. They knew far better than I did what the real issues were and so I did not want to muddy their waters. At the same time, however, I did want them to be able to get a feel for what an appreciative conversation is like, so that they could feel confident in the choice of their questions.

The trial conversations went well, with everyone complaining that they had not had enough time to explore it at the depth they would have liked. The reversed-roles session was, as is often the case, less gripping because both interviewer and interviewee had lost the shock of the new. On the other hand, it gave them a chance to get into the depth they thought they had been denied in the first session.

Based on their own experience, they had no difficulty under-standing what is meant by generative questions: indeed they seemed to come very naturally to them. Nor, because they had an intense shared interest in the subject, did they need much coaching in active listening. (See chapter 9.)

It was now time for me to take a back seat and allow the group to get into the substance of the inquiry. They understood the task well enough and were highly motivated. Now it was up to them to perform. As if to symbolize the transition, I left the table and stood with my back to the group looking out of the window.

I was delighted with how quickly they got to work, without any formal discussion of roles. They agreed that each person would spend twenty minutes producing a list of not less than four generative questions and not more than six. They would then pool them and identify the "best." (I had difficulty not interfering by asking what they thought they meant by the "best." They would have to face that question when the time came.)

They ended up with 27 questions, some very close to each other and some either factual or too vague for use. To save time, I volunteered to go through the list and eliminate the ones that were clearly unsuitable. Andrew, the accounts clerk, agreed to work with me, identifying the obvious overlaps and repetitions. It did not take us long to reduce the list to thirteen. I left the group to make their selection.

They were torn between the specific: questions that focused on particular elements of the church's life, such as the stewardship campaign or the summer camps; and the general; such questions as: "Tell me a story about when St. Luke's has been really important to you." They were worried that if the questions were too general, no themes would emerge so that it would become impossible to use the data in any strategic sense. But Andrew pointed out that by casting the questions in too specific a form, they would be confining the discussion to too narrow a canvas. After a long debate, in which a compromise of some general and some specific questions was suggested, they turned to me for advice. I was determined not to encourage that kind of dependency. It was their inquiry: they must make all the key decisions.

I sought to help them by taking them back to basics. "What are you hoping to get out of this?" I asked. Dick, the senior elder, came back as quick as a flash. "A vision. A sense of direction that is realistic and consistent with our past and our present."

"And where is that vision going to come from?"

There was a long pause. Eventually, Evelyn, the unmarried mother, said: "I guess different people will look in different directions. For me it will come from God, acting through his people here. Don't ask me how that works, because I don't know. I just kinda feel that God is in this process somewhere and it's our job to find Him." She looked almost embarrassed.

"That's right." Andrew was quick to throw her a life line. "And if God's in here somewhere, we don't want to set limits to what He can reveal. I mean we never could set limits anyway, but we don't want to . . . Gee, you guys know what I mean."

Sam came in, quietly. "OK. So everything's up for grabs. So let's make the questions as broad and open as we can. I guess I've changed my mind."

I record this dialogue in detail because it illustrates a very important dynamic at work. Perhaps because of the way I had lead the earlier sessions, the group was in danger of forgetting who—*Who* —was really running this inquiry. Over-anxious about getting the technicalities right, they had wavered in their perception that this was a deeply spiritual process of waiting on the Lord. They had therefore been lured into taking too much as given; into drawing the circle too small. Evelyn, with her interest in spirituality, had been the one whose great gift to the group had been to recall them to a fundamental faith in the activity of God, in the person of the Holy Spirit, guiding his people in their journey.

Having been so recalled, the group now wondered whether all the questions were not too narrow, especially if they were going to include in the interviewees people who were not active members of the church. After further long discussion, now carried on with much banter and good humor, they produced the following list:

1. What is the happiest memory you have of your time at St. Luke's? (or the church you currently attend?)

2. When do you think St. Luke's or any other church comes closest to what God wants it to be? Tell me a story about that.

3. If you were a non-Christian but someone alive to the spiritual values of life, what would you find most attractive about the church?

4. Can you tell me when you personally have felt nearest to God? When have your family or closest friends?

5. If Jesus walked into church next Sunday, what do you think would give him the greatest pleasure? If he walked in on a Sunday in five years time, what new developments would most excite him?

As a first trial I suggested that they spend the last hour of our time together trying out the questions on each other. This was not a fair or adequate test, of course, and would need to be followed by a bigger trial within the next few days, but it would get them familiar with the feel of the questions, as both askers and respondents.

As I had half-expected, it appeared from this preliminary trial that questions 2 and 5 were the ones that gripped people. In a way that worried me, because they were one step removed from the individual's own experience. Or so it seemed at first sight. When I listened more attentively to the answers, however, I realized that what was happening was that people were in fact talking about themselves and their own experiences, but were coding that in talk about what Jesus would or would not say or do (question 5).

It remained for us to decide whom to include apart from church members, the wider "stakeholders." The conversation veered between casting the net so wide the voices of the members would be drowned; and keeping it too tight so that we would pick up little new information or sense of perspective. In the end, the group decided to include ten members from each of the other churches in our part of town, four teachers from the three public schools, and (somewhat to my surprise) six storekeepers in the area. That would make about 40 additional interviews and about 20% of the likely total. I suspect none of us felt wholly comfortable; but it was a decision everyone could live with.

When I left them that evening, the group members were justifiably well satisfied with the progress they had made and were impatient to start the conversations with the members of the church. I suspect they thought me tiresomely academic when I insisted that they give the protocol a further trial, perhaps talking with a couple of people each and then comparing notes about how the process had gone, not worrying too much at this stage about the substance of the findings. "Remember," I said: "Your first question sets the tone for the whole of the conversation and therefore for the whole of the inquiry."

We booked a conference call to discuss what they had found. I could tell immediately how excited they were and found I had to push quite hard to get them to be critical of their protocol. Eventually they, or more particularly Sam, Evelyn and Andrew, agreed that the question about an individual's most intense religious experience was difficult to ask because it seemed to stop the flow, pushing people back into memories of bereavement, adolescent trauma or, in one case, of the recovery from rape.

"It's a huge privilege to listen," said Andrew, "and I was deeply touched that people I don't know that well should let all this stuff out, but I am not sure it is congruent with what we are doing. Maybe if people need to talk about it, and in one case that was the feeling I had, it will come out anyway, but we shouldn't put people under this kind of pressure?"

They decided to remove it.

"What of question 3, the non-Christian one?" I asked.

"Dynamite," said Dick. "I am converted and apologize for being a grouch about it. It gave people a chance to look wider. To ask themselves what we look like to the people we should be attracting. My only fear about it is that it may generate a lot of criticism. I'm not frightened of criticism. Perhaps we need it, but I'm not sure how that will square with the appreciative approach."

I too had wondered about this. It's the familiar insider/outsider dynamic. If an insider asks an outsider what he likes about the inside, the insider will hear the sub-text: "But there are other things I so dislike that I am staying outside."

"Try turning it round," I suggested. "Something like: If we were really keen on attracting non-members who are alive to spiritual values, what aspects of our life should we highlight? You can improve the wording, but you get the idea? Sure, it is important to get people to think about the non-members, but maybe some phrasing like that will make it easier to hold them in appreciative mode."

The conversation turned to how they would train the fifteen additional interviewers they reckoned they would need to cover the whole membership and the forty non-members without giving any-one too burdensome a load. The experience of drafting and then testing the protocol had given them more insight into the crucial importance of this training. They knew for themselves what they would have found hard to hear from me: that a mechanical plough-ing-through of the questions would be the kiss of death to the whole process. How, then, to ensure that the fifteen trainees came to the task with the openness, the prayerfulness and the insight that the work group were so rapidly acquiring?

A prior question, as Sam reminded us, was how to choose the fifteen. They agreed to ask the pastor if they could talk to the Sunday congregation about their experience so far in the sermon slot, thus emphasizing the Christ-centeredness of the process. "I figure," said Andrew, "that if we can convey the excitement and the potential we are beginning to get into touch with . . . wow! That will do it. We shall have volunteers lining up to help."

And so it turned out. There were more volunteers than spaces. To my delight it was Dick who decided unilaterally that preference should be given to the younger volunteers over the seniors. "Sorry I didn't have time to consult you guys," he said. "But (with a big grin) I guess you will have to trust me."

The training issue was still only half-resolved. I was resisting the invitation to come down and give a training day, because I was confident that the work group could do it; and would themselves learn much by doing so.

It was at this point that Eva, the college student who had hitherto been quiet, and, I felt, somewhat ill at ease, came into her own. She turned out to be a natural organizer/trainer, skillful at creating and adapting exercises that quickly built up peoples confidence while leaving them much to think about. For example, she realized that it was crucial for the interviewers to try to keep in appreciative mode. She therefore developed an exercise in which she interviewed Andrew (on a quite different and zany topic) and the trainees were expected to raise a red card everytime she shifted out of appreciative mode into analytical mode. After two evening sessions, all fifteen said they were ready to start.

One question that still bugged them was that of recording the answers. This is always an issue (see chapter 9), and I long ago accepted that there is no perfect solution. They agreed to keep very short notes during each interview but to leave themselves time to write up much more extended notes immediately after the end of the interview, "even if we have to go to the john to do so," said Evelyn. Quite.

At last, the real inquiry began, nearly three months after Peter's letter arrived on my desk. As I waited for the first reports of progress, I reflected that it now really was up to the Holy Spirit. I knew Peter had begun a small prayer cell, formed from some members of his Spirituality Workshop, that was meeting at 6:30 A.M. every morning to pray for the church as a whole. As I accepted the same discipline for myself, I knew that was the power house that was going to drive this whole exercise forward. It could not fail It might generate strange or even unwelcome messages, but they would be messages we needed to hear. I was impatient to hear what they were.

Chapter 6

Appreciative Inquiry in Action

Asking the questions

It was Peter who called me.

"I spent the evening with the work group," he began. "They've got about 240 interviews in. Some people, mostly those outside the church, are unwilling to do it. Some are away. There are probably about another 40 that are in principle doable. They want to know what to do now. I told them to hang on for a few more days, try to get the last few, and then wait until they hear from you."

"How do they feel about it?," I asked, keen to get into the real meat of the conversation rather than the administrative detail.

"Apart from one or two disasters, with people seeing it as an opportunity to slag off me, the church, God, and everything in between, they are pleased. No, more than pleased. Moved and excited, especially by how well the interviews with nonmembers went. I think the most crucial process question is whether they should carry on as a work group of the original five or incorporate all, or as many as want it, of the interviewers. I think Sam thinks that the interviewers now have such an investment in the whole thing; and know what their interviewees have said in a way that does not always come through in the notes, that it would be a pity to lose them as a resource at the interpretation and planning stage. What do you think?"

"If that's what they want, fine. My only concern would be the obvious one of the work group getting too big. It is supposed to be a work-group and you know what they say about maximum numbers for effective work? How many would want to join the work group?"

"At the moment probably all of them. They seem very possessive of "their interviewees." I think they are worried that the work group won't give them proper weight unless they, the interviewers, are there to champion their views, or at least tell their stories."

"That makes me nervous. What I suggest is a compromise. Get the work group to ask them in, say three or four at a time, to go through their data, share their stories, make any comments, observations they think pertinent, but leave the work group in control. They are a cracking group, working together really well. I think it would be a mistake to confuse the dynamic they have got going."

Identifying the themes

"The other thing they are beginning to worry about," Peter continued, " is how to handle the vast amount of stuff they have got. I reckon there's the best part of 2,000 pages of material. Say eight fair size novels. That's a lot of stuff for these folk, none of whom, with the possible exception of Eva, are academics. Even the intrepid Sam is beginning to quake a bit."

"I think it is important to take it gently, by stages. If they try to move too fast, they'll just get mental indigestion. Tell them to think of a three stage process. First, each member of the work group reads the reports of say 40 interviews of which roughly ten will be their own. So it's only 30 new ones. They may well need to read them through a couple of times. Then it's a good idea to make notes on any major themes that emerge. I will be very surprised if these do not almost self-select. They usually come through pretty unambiguously, but tell them to keep an eye open for the surprises; to be ready to be taken in the flank by the unexpected. It's not just routine majority-voting; it's being alert to the leading of the Spirit, and sometimes that is the voice of the people; sometimes it's the voice of the odd-ball prophet. They have to be alert to both possibilities."

"Having read and inwardly digested their original 40, they swap with someone else in the work group and read another 40. And so on. Same process. Read them at least twice—with eyes open. Make short notes. Then, in the third stage, they are ready to compare notes and try to distill themes that seem to come through. They may well find there are too many to handle properly, but we can talk again when they get to that stage."

I asked Peter how the early morning prayer-vigils were going. I still saw this, and Peter's patient exploration of the nature of the church in his teaching ministry in the liturgy at St. Luke's, as the spiritual core of the whole inquiry.

"I'm glad you ask about that," said Peter. "Because something really significant is going on there. The first week or two felt kinda heavy, like running thigh-deep in concrete. Gradually it's changed. There's a lightness, an en-joy-ment, a sense that I think all five of us share that, first, this is the most important hour of the day, but also that it's the most fun. And another thing. If one of us has to miss it for any reason, because someone is sick or has had to be out of town overnight on business or whatever, the rest of us feel bereaved, as though an important part of our own physical bodies has dropped off. It's almost weird. I've been interested in spirituality and prayer for a long time, but I have never known a group like this. Er, does this . . . I mean is this normal?"

I had to laugh at this gifted teacher of styles of prayer asking such a question.

"Yep. Perfectly. Not universal. Not mechanically guaranteed. But by no means abnormal. If people are bonded by real prayer for the body of Christ in their own community, it is not surprising if that Christ honors their prayer by being among them as they pray . . . But I don't need to teach you that."

"No, it's just that it's so . . . well, extraordinary."

I laughed again. "Ah, well that depends on the boundaries of the normal . . . and the teaching, the sermons. How's that going over?"

"Hard to say. You know how difficult it is to divine what people really think, or, much more, actually internalize. The stuff on the church as a prophetic community reverberated a good deal. I think that was a new idea to many of them, and not just the older folk. Some had difficulties with the idea of themselves as prophets, which I suspect means they at least half-misunderstood what I was getting at. But at least they are still talking about it, and that was over a month ago."

"Well, in one sense the proof of the pudding will be in the interviews. We'll have to see what comes through them. If one of the themes to emerge is that St. Luke's needs to develop a prophetic ministry, you'll know you have been heard right enough!"

I later heard from Sam that Peter's call had been prompted by a near-crisis in the work group. Eva and Dick, especially, had become overwhelmed by the size of the task ahead of them. They felt they were in danger of drowning in paper and could see no way through or past the piles of notes that were accumulating on their own desks and they knew on twenty other desks through the church. Interestingly, they had expressed their anxiety in terms of anger with me—for "getting them into this mess and then disappearing." Such a reaction was no surprise: but it did suggest that Peter's role of "occasional consultant" to the group was not working at the emotional level, however satisfactory it might have been at the factual, rational level.

The work group would need more effective "containing" or "holding" than Peter could give it, especially as he was, rightly, anxious to keep his (emotional) distance from the work group. On reflection I counted myself lucky that the anger had been directed at me: I was safely out of the way and was not emotionally or organizationally involved. It would have been much more damaging if it had been directed at Sam or Peter, the two obvious targets.

To try to avoid this kind of emotional turmoil which could be seriously threatening to the effectiveness of the group, I decided to take a risk and gave Evelyn a call. I explained the issues to her and asked her to accept responsibility within the group for getting people to put their feelings on the table.

"Don't try to turn it into group therapy," I said. "That's not what it's about. But just get them to tell each other how they are feeling and encourage them to accept each others' statements. They don't need to agree. But they do need to listen. So if someone is frustrated or frightened or fed up, they can be heard. It's not hugely sophisticated stuff, but it will help them when they get into some of the tougher material. And don't let them back off from telling how they feel about each other, so long as they do so honestly but courteously."

To my great relief, Evelyn saw the point immediately.

"Yeah," she said. "We need somewhere to put some of how we are feeling. And the only place we can put it safely right now is with each other. I'll do my best."

As the work group moved, over the next weeks, towards creating the provocative propositions that would define the parameters of the strategic plan, Evelyn did better than her best and gave them the kind of support on the emotional level that Peter's early morning prayer group was already giving them on the spiritual level. Purists, I knew, would say it was too little and too late, and I had to live with the guilt of that charge. But at least we had stuck a finger in that particular dike.

Having made these adjustments, I was content to let the work group proceed with reading the interviews through and distilling themes. That it would take time and effort was clear: what I think the members of the work group had not adequately anticipated was the effect on them of reading this material in concentrated bursts.

"It was an astonishing experience," Evelyn told me later. "Like . . . oh, I don't know . . . like listening in at a confessional under a high pressure jet. Or perhaps seeing into the heart of dozens of people and watching them break . . . Or . . . No, that's all too negative. It wasn't a negative experience. Far from it. It was a great and enriching experience. I was overwhelmed by this amazing wealth of the experience of God's goodness and graciousness, and a longing to . . . respond, almost to be worthy of it. That's where the heart-break and the 'if only' comes from: people realizing that we are missing so many tricks by being so human!"

After two weeks work on the data, the group met to pool their list of themes. Sam called me late that night. She was so exhausted but so euphoric I could not keep coherent notes of our conversation, but the gist was clear enough. What surprised everyone was, first, the extent to which the same themes kept coming up but second how "way out" or oddball themes, the very unconventionality of which might have made them unique, found resonances from within the material. "They may be oddballs; but they are evidently not screw-balls" was the way Sam put it. She promised to e-mail me a complete list of themes which they had managed to shake down to seventeen at that evening's meeting.

Looking down them next morning, I was astonished by how few bore on the internal life of the church, and how many were, in one form or another, about its outreach. This was exactly the reverse of what I had expected. I had thought that what gave life and energy to that congregation was its own inner life; its sense of belonging to this little group; of knowing and being known. Yet the themes revealed that what gave the bulk of the congregation a sense of vitality and meaningfulness was less the "internal" life of the church than what they were doing or might be doing "externally." I rang Peter straight-away.

He shared my sense of surprise—and delight. For here were the seeds of a strategic plan that transcended anything that would have come out of the normal processes of planning with the existing groups of people. To make absolutely sure that we were on safe ground, we fixed a conference call with Sam and Dick to get their reading on how the themes had emerged.

They could add little apart from reassurance that the work group had not attempted to slant or bias the themes in any way. What struck me was that they were much less surprised, more laid back than Peter and I. "Well, I guess we have had the privilege of listening to the people, both directly and indirectly," said Dick. "It's a kind of cumulative process and I don't mean that you start to hear only what you have heard before. Obviously there is a danger of that, but we checked that out with each other in the work group and I am satisfied that was not operating. Nor do I think it is credible that one respon-dent was telling the next what they had said, so there was some kind of contamination. That's just not possible. No, I think what you are seeing is what people are saying, and that's both people in the church and outside it. They are interested in a major shift. Less time and effort on ourselves; and more time and effort on the needy in our own community and beyond. Obviously I'm putting it too starkly: there are a number of themes that relate to our worship, our teaching, our young. Especially our young. But I think you have identified the center of gravity aright."

Sam cut in. "When can you come down and help us with the next step? We are really keen now to move on from the themes to the provocative propositions. We see how important that is going to be and we don't want to make a mess of it."

"Come on, Sam," I replied. "You guys are not going to make a mess of it. I am certainly not going to come and hold your hands. You know what you need to do: frame propositions that will stretch you but which are, just, doable; and put them in the present tense. But before you get into that, you will have to reduce the list of themes, either by combining them (I think there are a few possibilities of that, but beware of combining the incompatible), or more likely, weeding them. Not easy. You will hate that. And avoid dropping the most exciting just because there are not too many stories about it. This is not a popularity poll: it's discernment. You may have to sit with them all quite a long time, going over the stories, getting to the "inside" of them, listening with the heart. Don't rush it."

I knew that Sam and Dick, and no doubt the rest of the work group, were anxious to keep up the momentum The last thing I wanted, however, was the work group feeling that they had to move faster to fend off external criticism.

"Having seen the list of themes," said Dick. "Do you have any idea of how many provocative propositions we ought to be aiming at?"

"Yuh! I don't really like that way of putting it, Dick. You have to let the stories speak for themselves. I certainly don't want to put limits on it at this stage. At the same time, you obviously have to have at the back of your mind how many propositions you will, as a church, be able to implement. It's pretty demoralizing having a long list of plans that you cannot carry out. So be open, but not so open that you end up with wholly unrealistic demands on your own capacity. I guess it's a fine judgment."

After the call was finished, I fell to thinking more about Peter. At one level, I was impressed by his courage. He had not shown any dismay or anxiety about the fact that it looked as if his church was about to commit itself to a major change in direction, and that a direction in which he was not specially gifted to travel. I guessed that his present sense of hopefulness and peace was firmly rooted in his prayer life and in the strength and support he was deriving from the early morning prayers that were of course continuing. At another level, I was unsure what to make of his passivity: was this too a reflection of a man of near-absolute trustfulness? Or was it a kind of subdued panic: a refusal to face the realities and rather choose to go on from day to day, hoping that he would somehow get through?

I knew that the next couple of weeks would reveal the answer.

Chapter 7

Provocative Propositions

Forming the Future

The work group worked on the seventeen themes, trying to reduce them by combination or elimination. Slowly, the number was gnawed away to fifteen, then to twelve.

Then they were stuck. "We listen to the stories behind the themes and one or other of us, sometimes more than one of us, says: 'That's right. That's too important. We cannot let that go.' It's almost a physical thing, as if something has hit you in the stomach." Evelyn sounded near to tears. "I have sort of fallen in love with these people and what they are telling us about their faith journey, their hopes, their sense of who they are. I cannot bear to let any of that just disappear."

She was telling me this in the context of a decision the group had arrived at the night before: that, next weekend, they would go into retreat and ask the early morning prayer group to join them. Clearly this was not a "retreat" in the sense that word is sometimes used in the business community, a chance to get away from the pressures of the work place and win time and space to think through problems. This was to be a retreat in the classical sense: a time to be in silence, in prayer, before God. I suspected that this had been Evelyn's own idea; but I was delighted that the prayer group had seen the need to bring together their experience of praying for the appreciative inquiry with the work that Evelyn and her colleagues had been doing on the data. We all had to trust that the retreat would, in its own way, open up a path through the difficulties that Evelyn had described in her own inimitable style.

Peter had agreed to go on the retreat; and, in doing so, had made only one stipulation: that conscious work on the inquiry be halted. He knew well enough that everyone, and especially the work group, would be involved in it at various levels of conscious and unconscious engagement, but he was determined that the sense of perspective, the sense of opening it up to God, of being available to the work of the Holy Spirit should not be crowded out by endless mental shaking of the data.

I thought it important to hold back at this point. "Let God be God" was the admonition of one of my own most influential spiritual directors; and here was the time to take that excellent advice.

It was Andrew who called me after their return: his first independent call to me and, it transpired, his first experience of a near-silent retreat of waiting on the Lord. He had evidently found it a deeply moving time.

"It's still too early to say how far we have moved," he said. "But I'll tell you one thing, if I can find an adequate way to put it into words. I certainly feel differently, and I guess the others would say the same. Less pressured. Less overwhelmed. More trusting. More, oh, I don't know . . . more ready to stand back and let God, the data, the people's own stories do the work. Does that make any sense to you? It's a difference in attitude, I suppose."

"It's also a big shift towards the real depth of the appreciative mode," I said. "It sounds as if you are no longer trying to analyze, to manipulate, shape, make coherent by forcing a pattern upon all that stuff. You are coming at it from a deeper part of yourself, the part perhaps where spirit resides."

61

There was a pause. "It's still going to be a difficult task," muttered Andrew.

I laughed. "Of course. The appreciative mode doesn't pretend to be a doddle. But you sound to me to be free in a way that you were not before. And it's exercising that freedom that will give you the way through you are looking for; and which will, too, give you all a lot of fun."

To capitalize on this new found sense of freedom, the work group decided that they would meet for two long sessions the week after the retreat and aim to have a preliminary list of provocative propositions by the end of the week. I was not sure that they were wise to drive themselves this hard, but I knew that I had to learn to trust their wisdom.

As they later told me, they were themselves surprised how smoothly the discussions went. They quickly agreed that the "growing point" was the emphasis on the outreach programs and that they should therefore be given priority. They also recognized, however, that growth demands a stem to act as a support and a channel of nutrition. In that spirit, they recognized that they needed to give attention to what gave life and energy to that "stem." Having reached that agreement, they went back to the stories. Each selected the three stories that, quite apart from their categorization in themes, gave them the greatest sense of hope, joy and spiritual engagement. Those formed the basis of the first shot at forming provocative propositions that would do justice to both "growing point" and "stem."

In their first crude state, a sample read like this:

St. Luke's nourishes its people to go out into the world to proclaim the goodness and forgiveness of God.

We are a people who seek to live prophetically, as if the kingdom has come. To do this we are trained and sustained in church, but the world is where our prophetic lives unfold.

We listen to God in the sacraments and Scriptures, but also in the voices of the hurt, the needy and the forsaken.

We sustain and are sustained by our young people: we welcome their vision and impatience with the status quo as they welcome our wisdom and experience.

St. Luke's is part of a wider network in this town and beyond it. We are true to ourselves only when we function with proper regard to our part in that network.

St. Luke's exists primarily for the people outside it. In all our activities, use of resources and proclamation, we honor that fact.

St. Luke's is an ark which shelters people who have been damaged and by accepting them unconditionally, reequips them to live and to love.

We take prayer seriously. We pray for the scarcely possible and thereby make it highly probable. And we pray more for others than we pray for ourselves.

We acknowledge that God is at work in his world and chooses as his prime expression his body, the Church. We therefore seek to be his Body, both broken and glorious. And we accept that the glory lies in the brokenness.

St. Luke's is committed to a journey in search of a fuller obedience. We need each other on that journey, but above all we need the grace and encouragement of God. To that end, we move out from a life of prayer and worship to search God out in the communities in which we live and work.

There were as many again, most of them reflecting the themes incorporated here: the interdependence of the inward and the outward; the centrality of prayer; the call to costly discipleship; the notion of the church as a cross between a recovery-room, a food-line and a class-room; the need to establish healthy dialogue between the various elements of the congregation; and the expectation of finding God "in all things." Immediately, I was struck by what was not here: nothing on the fabric, the choir, the debt, finance, church governance, the existing organizations of the church, the ministry of the clergy, the liturgy. Practically nothing, too, on the wider church and nothing, at least directly, on the missions. The focus seemed to be primarily on the quality of the relationship between St. Luke's and the wider community, expressed in relatively local terms. In other words, the issue was not "the world": it was "our world," as experienced in this town and its immediate environs.

I asked Dick to give me a flavor of the stories that lay behind this emphasis, one that I would never have predicted on the basis of my admittedly scant knowledge of this church. He gave me two that seemed to him to be in some sense central.

"There was this youngish woman, late thirties, I suppose. She was involved in a very messy divorce, being hounded by a violent husband. She wandered into St. Luke's out of desperation. She had never crossed the threshold before. I guess she was looking for peace, or sanctuary or space to get herself together. Perhaps even she did not know why she went in. Anyways, there she was, sitting in the corner by the front entrance, sobbing. Now Mary Saltern—you remember her, elderly lady, severe limp—was in the sanctuary tidying up, and heard this sobbing. She came out, saw the woman and without a word passing between them, just held her and let her sob till she could sob no more. She, the young woman, said it was one of the deepest, most God-revealing moments of her life—that a stranger could accept her so spontaneously, so unquestioning, at her weakest and most vulnerable. That to her was a revelation. I guess she hadn't had too much loving in her life up to then. Anyways, the story goes on and she ends up a regular member here. She's big on the summer camps. She does an amazing job with some of the people who come on that. I guess she knows what some of them are going through."

He was silent some moments as if wondering whether to say more. There was more to be said, but he shook his head and went on with the second story.

"An important businessman in town, right? Computers mostly, bulk supplies to schools, hospitals, state-wide. . Making a lot of money. Driving himself and his staff hard. Has a car smash, over the legal limit. So he's in pretty serious trouble. He's also in the hospital. Ribs broken. Leg broken. Whiplash in the spine. But he's a fighter. Soon as he can lift his head off the pillow, he's talking to his lawyer: how he's going to sue the guy he crashed into, the state police, the car makers, everyone. And he starts giving the nurses and doctors a hard time. Why can't they do this or that for him? Why can't he get up? If they were any good, they'd have him fixed up by now. You can imagine the drift. Anyways, into the next room goes Johnny Speight. He's only in his late twenties. Young wife. Two little girls, one still a baby. In initially for tests; then they find he has a brain tumor. Johnny gets to know the computer guy and though they are as different temperamentally as chalk and cheese they become friends.

"The computer guy pops in to see Johnny just after he's been told about the tumor. He's got to have a major operation. Very difficult. Very dangerous. Might work. Might make things worse. Johnny tells him all this and the guy is bowled over. Knocked flat. So Johnny ends up comforting him. Then Angela, Johnny's wife, comes in and they talk about it calmly, quietly. This is too much for the computer guy. 'What's the matter with you people?' he yells. 'You don't even seem concerned.' And it's Angela who takes him on."

"'We are concerned right enough,' she says, 'but that doesn't mean we have to be anxious or worried. Johnny is in God's hands. And he could not be anywhere safer. We are all in God's hands. Me and the girls, and you. For you, your business and your money and your being a mover and shaker are important. That's where you are. But with us it's not like that.' And she goes on to express a very simple but very profound faith that worldly success and wealth and prestige are not what it's all about. That what matters is trust and the knowledge of God in daily life."

"The computer guy doesn't know what to make of this. At first he blusters. Then he goes silent. Then he storms out. But when Angela has gone, he creeps back and asks Johnny if he, Johnny, really goes with all this. 'Sure' says Johnny: 'I'd be in the same state as you if I didn't.'"

"Anyways, three days later, the guy asks to talk to Angela again, and the next thing he's asking for the old pastor to go see him. You can guess the rest for yourself. Angela is a remarkable person. So quiet yet so strong. I don't think this guy had encountered strength like that before. He knew when he was licked. Now he's as gentle as a lamb. Gives huge amounts of money away. Lives very simply. You'd never guess he was one of the wealthiest men in town—for miles around, actually. He won't serve on the church board because he says he hasn't been a Christian long enough. But he's always there, every Sunday, usually helping clean up after the coffee and doughnuts. You'd never guess."

Having heard these stories, I began to read the draft provocative propositions in a new light. I could begin to see the commitment and the insight that lay behind their bland, unassuming exteriors. It seemed as if the people of St. Luke's were acknowledging that what gave them life, vitality and joy was being in touch with the deepest parts of other people's experiences, as though they discovered their own depths, their own meaningfulness when circumstances permitted them to glimpse the profoundest parts of others. I did not read this as a prurient voyeurism; but as a way of recognizing that it is in those profundities that God most readily reveals himself. "Out of the depths have I called unto thee" and the call is answered. Evidently what brought many members of the church alive was this search for depth, their own and other peoples: in revolt, perhaps, against the simplicities and superficialities with which most of us lead our lives most of the time. And if that was right, and it was still only a glimmer that needed careful testing, then the writing of the provocative propositions that would form the base of the strategic plan needed to sharpen and focus that central issue. For it was beginning to sound as if many of the interviewees were calling for a more mature, more spiritually-aware church life than Peter, Sam or I had yet dreamed of.

The work group clearly had a lot more work to do, sharpening the shape of the provocative propositions and reducing their number. I shared my impressions with them, as someone who had heard only a couple of stories and whose judgment may therefore be worthless. "The issue is not whether I am right or wrong; but whether you are now in a position to go deeper in yet: to see beyond these draft propositions and the stories that generated them, to see into . . . well, to see into the soul of the church and work from there. You are very close to that, I believe. We have traveled a long way since all this began. One more heave."

"OK. But how?"

"There's no magic answer to that. In the end discernment is a gift. But one thing you could do— it might be helpful or it might not, judge for yourselves—is to look at the propositions you have and ask yourselves, first individually; then in pairs and then as a whole group: What deep need is this proposition seeking to meet? If it is not clear to you, that might suggest that the proposition is ripe for dropping. Or substantial redrafting."

They went to work and I kept in touch with Peter almost daily. I talked about the way things seemed to me to be moving and tried to interpret his reaction. Initially, I was not sure whether it was relief or excitement or dread: he is not always an easy person to read. He was struck by how much more radical the group seemed to be becoming, not in a populist, political sense, but in the deeper sense of getting to the root of matters. That led him to see how everything in the church might have to be redesigned, rethought, reassessed.

Eventually he said: "Oddly, I'm not scared of that. If this is coming from the real spiritual experience of our people, out of their discovery of where God is for them, then it will be a fantastic leap forward. We may stumble, but we've got to take it, and trust in God to pull us through in exactly the same way as he has thus far."

By the end of the week, the work group had produced a list of propositions they were ready to put to the church as a whole. They read like this:

1. St. Luke's is inclusive. It comprises people at different stages of their spiritual pilgrimage and sustains, nourishes and encourages them all. We recognize that it is in the meeting of people's deepest need, inside and outside the church, that we are often enabled to make progress in our own journeys and for that reason we give a high priority to a corporate life of reflective service to those around us.

2. We see prayer and worship as central pillars of that reflective service; and we are therefore committed to a liturgical life that honors God, sustains his people and stretches us in our life of discipleship.

3. We value all our members, whatever their status, their gifts and their input. We recognize the privilege of having younger people and people of color join in the life of the church and we make as creative use of their gifts as they will permit.

4. We are proud of our links with the wider community and we extend them, especially to the needy, vulnerable and neglected among us. Recognizing the limits on our own resources, we encourage, enable and collaborate with other agencies, whether Christian or not, which serve the disadvantaged in ways we are unable to do directly.

5. We recognize that discipleship is a life long calling, and entails life long learning. As a church we provide learning opportunities for all our members; and as individuals, we accept our obligation to make the most of those opportunities.

6. We appreciate the ministry of our ordained clergy; and we acknowledge that ministry is exercised in the name of the whole church. It is complemented by effective lay leadership and we therefore encourage, by all the means available to us, the development of such leadership.

I recognized how much hard work, tough discussion and old-fashioned horse-trading had gone into reducing the propositions to this manageable number and scope—not least by the tell-tale signs of overlap and roughness of wording. So far from regretting these, I welcomed them as evidence that the work group had refrained from endless word-smithing which might have ironed out some of the creases, but which would have left too smooth a final product. The rough edges would command attention. (They would also attract the attention of every would-be drafter in the church, but that was a pressure that would have to be handled later.)

I told the work group they had done a fine job, and left them to plan a suitable way of reporting their conclusions to the church at large. As I waited to hear their plans, I prayed that Peter's brave words about going with the process in the conviction that the Holy Spirit was at work in it were still alive for him. The next couple of weeks would put them to the test.

Chapter 8

Consensus Building and Planning

Sharing the dream

The work group decided that to honor the fact that they had been aware of the spiritual significance and meaningfulness of their work, they needed to present the propositions to the church in the context of worship. There was no time to organize a special event, so they agreed with Peter that their presentation, and the retelling (in suitably anonymous form where that was appropriate) of some of the key stories, would take the place of the sermon. The church board and the stewardship group undertook jointly to contact every family on the members roll personally to underline the importance of the event.

From the process point of view, I was a little uneasy about separating the presentation from the consensus-building. There were two issues here. The first was that by presenting the propositions in so formal and solemn a setting, there was a risk that they would be thought to be unalterable. The second was that while such a formal presentation might make the consensus- building easier in a superficial sense, there was a real danger that people would buy into the propositions out of a sense of obligation or awe, rather than out of genuine conviction and commitment. That would render sterile, or worse, the whole operation.

I therefore told Dick and Sam, the two people I could quickly raise on the phone, that they needed to give some thought to how they were going to handle the consensus building.

"Yep," said Dick, as though he had been expecting my objections. "We already thought of that. We shall give everyone a copy of the propositions, with two related stories for each proposition. There will be a quiet time at the end of the service when they can read those. Then we'll get them into groups of about half a dozen, more or less where they are sitting, to brainstorm on the propositions and pick out the two that most accurately reflect the reactions of the group as a whole. In other words, which two of the six have the highest 'Wow! Ye-e-e-s-s!' factor. And we will give each group a 'torpedo card.' If all the people in the group agree, they can torpedo any one proposition by holding up their card. But they can only torpedo one, and only if they all agree. In theory, with something like 30-odd groups, we could get a lot of torpedoes flying around and the whole lot of the propositions could be sunk. If that happens . . . well, we'll have had a good time! Equally, we shall probably find that every proposition is endorsed by at least some groups."

As their thinking developed from this early conversation with Dick, the group came up with a more elaborate plan. After the process Dick had described, they would make available, in the middle of the church, a supply of glue and cardboard and bits of wood and "all the kinds of construction junk you can think of," as Evelyn put it. Each group of church members which had identified their most favored propositions would then be asked to model them using the junk available. The models would be presented to the congregation as a whole and then offered on the altar in a short service of dedication. The most gripping of the models would be kept in the church hall as a constant reminder of the priorities and self-understanding of the church as a whole.

"We think when people have had to work on the ideas with their hands," said Evelyn: "To really feel the texture and fabric of what the propositions are all about, they will get a hold of them in quite a new way. Sure they will be a bit apprehensive when they start. But they'll get into it. You bet. And what matters is not that they create a work of art, but that they try. At least it's something they will remember and talk about for a long time!"

I was able to be present for the service the following Sunday. The church was fuller than usual—I guessed around 70% of the member families were represented. Realistically, that was about as high as one could expect, but I regretted not having suggested that they plan this occasion ahead. (I later reversed this judgment. It became clear during the day that it was the spontaneity of the occasion that was a large part of its special appeal.)

The congregation was held by the retelling of the stories. The work group had put a lot of effort into presenting them effectively, telling some with one voice, and others with different voices for different parts. The sense of the accumulation of God's presence with his people in this church and this community was so intense that the end of the stories was not, as one might have expected, accompanied by polite applause but by a profound, prayerful silence. From that it seemed natural and appropriate to move directly into the passing of the peace and the celebration of the Last Supper, with Peter cleverly incorporating the appreciative inquiry into the Blessing of the Gifts: "Through your goodness we have this bread . . . Through your goodness we have this wine . . . Through your goodness we have the outcome of this inquiry, work of our hearts and minds, the incarnation of your presence with us. It will help us become the Body of Christ." There was a suitably firm response from the congregation: "Blessed be God for ever."

I wandered round eaves-dropping on the multitude of little huddles round the church, trying to garner an impression of the reactions. Initially, it was disappointing with people saying: "Yeah. Fine. But how? What does it mean in practical terms?" Slowly they began to shift beyond that facile reaction and concentrate on what was involved in each proposition: what its many layers of meaning were disclosing; how its implementation would revolutionize the life of the church as they knew it. The volume of the buzz began to rise. Four groups began to talk about using the torpedo: three against the proposition about young people and people of color; the other against the proposition about working with non-Christian service groups in the community. Both were entirely predictable—and correctly predicted by Sam—but, more surprisingly, neither revolt was led by obvious elderly conservatives. Neither secured the necessary unanimity. The torpedoes stayed out of sight. The opposition would, nonetheless, need careful handling in the months ahead.

The model construction exercise worked far better than I had dared hope. Certainly a few of the groups—no more than three or four—found it hard to get into, but even they produced something. Most groups threw themselves into it with huge verve, some ignoring the refreshments that appeared half way through. The final products were an impressive blend of the surreal, the witty, the bizarre and the ingenious. One, illustrating the (controversial) proposition on youth and people of color, drew spontaneous and prolonged applause for its combination of clever design and meticulous workmanship. A multicolored figurine in wood, paper and fabric, it caught exactly the exaggerated confidence and carelessness of a teenager's gait as it led a motley gaggle of smaller figures up a winding path.

As Dick had predicted, none of the propositions was unrepresented in the final display, though it looked as if the one on life-long learning was least popular, perhaps because it implied an immediate commitment to make use of learning opportunities. Peter conducted the dedication with simplicity, humor and a prayerfulness that well caught the mood of the moment. We were serious about what we were doing; but we did not need to be solemn about it.

Planning for Action

I met with the work group later that afternoon: they were well satisfied with their reception and with the enthusiasm with which the members of the church had entered the process. "It's unstoppable," said Eva. "This place will never be the same again. We've just got to get the next steps right."

That was indeed the issue. We now had the strategic plan in embryo: it still had to be brought to term and given birth. I was unsure that the work group was the ideal instrument for that process. First they were exhausted by what they had achieved already, and although they were highly motivated, they were not necessarily the best people to shape the propositions into action plans that were fully costed, programmed and integrated for the next five years. I raised that point with them.

They were clearly unhappy about pulling out of the process now. "I don't want to be possessive about it," said Andrew. "But the fact is that we know what lies behind each proposition , and we have a pretty shrewd idea what each entails. Sure, we need help. Sure, we are tired. Sure, we need to involve a wider circle. But I for one would be very . . . well, let's say saddened to be hoofed out of the business now."

Even Evelyn, for whom I knew the last few weeks had been an immense strain, given all her other responsibilities, shared this intense sense of ownership. I spoke openly of my anxiety that they would dominate any wider group and impede any reshaping of the strategy implied, as they saw it, in the propositions. They took the point, but argued that they could work collaboratively with a wider group, listening to and learning from their reactions to the practicalities of putting the propositions into action.

It was not, of course, my decision. It was a matter for the church board. Led by Dick, the board decided to ask the whole work group to join them to form the plans based on the provocative propositions. There were thus nearly twenty lay people on what came to be known, in only half conscious self-parody, as the Planning Commission. It was their task to tease out the propositions into specific action plans, assigning executive authority, a budget, a line of accountability and an evaluative process to each and then integrate them into a seamless unity of purpose and action which would run over the next five years.

In some ways, this was a straightforward exercise in resource allocation and priority setting. In two other dimensions, it was quite different from the way in which these standard disciplines would be applied in a business environment. First, the Commission agreed very early in its deliberations that it needed to honor the prayerfulness in which the appreciative inquiry had been carried out. While it was impractical for the whole Commission to continue the 6:30 A.M. vigils everyday, they agreed that on the days surrounding each meeting of the Commission as many people as could would meet at the church at 7:00 A.M. for a period of prayer. Half of these sessions would be silent; the other half would be led, focusing directly on the current work of the Commission.

Second, the Commission, unprompted by the old appreciative inquiry work group, recognized that it needed to keep alive the spirit of the appreciative inquiry, constantly refocusing on the sources of energy, vitality and spiritual enrichment even as they wrestled with resource scarcities and all the minutiae of detailed planning. They hit on two ways of doing that. Each meeting of the Commission would start by one member of the appreciative inquiry work group retelling one of the stories from the inquiry. And one of the criteria they would use when assessing options for the programmatic expression of the propositions would be: How is this idea consistent with what enables people to feel in tune with God? In these two ways, they hoped to shift the central focus of all their planning from the old paradigm of problems, deficits and scarcities to the appreciative paradigm of "best practice" and opportunities. "We can't ban the word *problem*," said Dick. "But we can make sure we use it as little as possible. We need to look at what God is doing and how he is doing it and go with that."

As the main focus of this volume is on appreciative inquiry and its use in strategic planning, I do not need to recite at the same length the detailed steps of the planning process. Let me concentrate, rather, on the way in which the Commission managed to stay with the appreciative mode over the next couple of months.

Many of its members paid tribute to the role of the stories, both at the start of their meetings and as incorporated in their shared prayer vigils. It was less that the stories recreated the atmosphere of the consensus building arena; more, I think, that they recalled the Commission to the fundamentals of what they were doing. For most of the stories were, in one way or another, about how people had become more aware of the presence of God in their lives. Sometimes that was made overt; many times it was more subtly implied. In each case, however, as recounted in the context of the Commission's work, they acted as a reminder that the essence of the Commission's purpose was to discern where God was already at work and bring the efforts of the church into line with that. The spiritual and psychic difference made by such a shift in emphasis is as hard to exaggerate as it is to express in concrete terms. One illustration will have to suffice.

The Commission broke into working parties to tackle each proposition. One such got itself into a tangle over the forms of collaboration with external agencies. A particular issue became how the church could collaborate with a Jewish organization in town (there was a large Jewish population to the West of the town) which was caring for babies—of all racial and religious backgrounds—which were HIV positive. The organization was ready to accept help from St. Luke's, providing it was neither conditional nor labeled in any way. Everyone accepted that this was a high priority in terms of social need. Yet some took the view, perfectly rationally, that, given the scarcity of resources, both financial and personal, it was more effective to work closely with a church sponsored orphanage in town, some of whose children were indeed HIV positive youngsters. "At least we can then sail under our true colors," said someone. "We shall be meeting the same need, but doing so openly as a Christian witness."

The Christian operation was already well funded and resourced. The Jewish scheme was run on half a shoestring. The greater need was obvious enough. Need or witness? It is an old conundrum. Positions began to harden. A former nurse in her late fifties, a member of the church board who tended to the conservative wing of opinion, asked exactly the right question of the woman who had visited both projects to gather information and explore the possibilities of collaboration:

"From what you saw and what you felt, where would you say those babies are most loved. Physically, I mean. Picked up and cuddled? Cherished for their short lives? Made to feel they are accepted and valued, small mites as they are?"

The researcher had no hesitation: "In the Jewish clinic."

"Then that's where the spirit of Christ is and that's where we ought to be," concluded the nurse, abruptly but serenely reversing her own position.

I may be wrong, but I strongly suspect that question would not have been asked—and its answer would not have had the same force—if the church had not been exposed to the appreciative approach.

Finance is always an area where churches find it hard to remain faithful. The anxious bean counting mentality is always waiting to reassert itself, often with destructive results. How far was it true, then, that in the case St. Luke's, the internalization of the appreciative approach enabled the Commission to transcend financial anxieties without becoming careless or irresponsible?

Clearly one of the Commission's fundamental tasks was precisely to match resources of all sorts, including finance, to the programs under development. Inevitably, there came the crunch point where more of this meant less of that. No appreciative approach in the world can avoid those hard trade-offs. What it can do is enable the decision-making group to see beyond that trade-off to the spiritual reality behind it. And I find that this has two effects. First, it sometimes stimulates lateral thinking that removes or softens the trade-off. And second, it enables the tone of the conversation in which these issues are discussed to be more creative, open and sensitive. Let me give an example.

An obvious approach to the budgeting side of the Commission's work would have been to take a decision about how much of their income to spend on outreach and how much to spend on "internal" matters such as stipends and wages, office, choir, fabric and so on. They knew what they were already spending on such costs and so it was notionally easy to project those costs forward and see how much would be left for outreach; or how much extra money would have to be raised for a credible outreach program to be put in place. That, I suggest, would have been a "normal," "sensible," "business-like" way of going about their work. It is one they rejected as soon as it was suggested.

It was someone who had been most resistant to the whole appreciative inquiry approach who was most vehement in declaring "the old way" redundant.

"That's just what we don't want to be doing," he said. "Surely if we are going to be faithful to the appreciative method and all that it has taught us about being appreciative of the goodness of God, we need to start with where he is at work in our community and our church and work from there. That will almost certainly mean that we want to spend more than we are currently raising, the great services of the Stewards notwithstanding. Well, if that's where we come out, we need to look at that in the light of where the Spirit is leading us.

We might have to risk a deficit. We might have to increase the debt. We might have to sell off some church plant. I don't know. But what I can't accept is that we approach this planning exercise in exactly the same way that we have approached all the earlier planning, or pseudo-planning, exercises we've ever got involved in. Otherwise we have wasted the last eight weeks." Murmurs of agreement showed that he was by no means a lone voice.

As he had predicted, they did indeed find that the implementation of the provocative propositions would cost more than their current revenue, by a factor of nearly two. Yet, as he had also implied, that was not considered an argument for trimming the programs. With the dissent of two of the Stewardship group, who clearly (but erroneously) thought that they were under criticism for not having raised more money, the Commission took three major decisions. The first was to rent the church hall to a nursery school that was looking for new premises. The second was to simplify and streamline the administration, with the result that there would be no need to replace one of the two secretaries (who was leaving to start a family.) So far, so conventional. The third step they took, however, was to engage the whole community in an appreciative-inquiry based fund-raising effort for the three most high-visibility components of the outreach program: the work with HIV babies; the proposed "Saturday Club" for the children of one parent families; and a small rehab unit for released prisoners (to be run in conjunction with a United Methodist church on the far side of town.)

Instead of going out to fund-raise in the normal "selling" mode, the plan was to engage donors across the community, from the few large companies to individual households, in an appreciative approach to their own community. By asking such questions as: What do you care about in this community?; What makes you feel good about this town?; When do you think we as a community are at our best?; they expected to enable potential donors to share their vision of a community that cared for its most needy and most neglected. Where there is vision, they were confident there would be money, and much more than money. For at a deeper level, they knew that this was likely to prove a more effective way of revealing the presence of Christ among his people than traditional methods of "selling" the gospel.

"If we can bring that off," Dick said, "bringing together the outreach and the witness in a way that enables people to capture a glimpse of what we think we have glimpsed, the money will look after itself and, much more important, the church will grow in numbers and faithfulness. It's a heck of a tall order. But I think we have a better than even chance of doing it."

Three years on, I can report that Dick's faith was not misplaced.

Chapter 9

Running Your Own Appreciative Inquiry

This chapter is an extended commentary on the St. Luke's case study. It is intended to enable readers who want to conduct their own appreciative inquiry to understand at greater depth some of the issues of process that emerged in the last four chapters, so that in their own work they will be aware of some of the strategic choices that have to be made as the inquiry develops. To put the issues I shall raise in context, I have indicated the relevant pages from the St. Luke's study. Lest that be misunderstood, let me emphasize again that this process can be applied to any church-related organization: from service organizations to hierarchical structures like diocesan offices or synods. I have concentrated on the congregational level because I am confident that is where it will be applied most often: but it has much to offer to all branches and levels of the church's life.

1. Integration, or getting it all together (pp. 49f, 53)

In some ways this is the most important issue of all. Although appreciative inquiry is used in all kinds of secular organizations, its use in church settings is especially appropriate because it points directly to the work of the Holy Spirit in the life of the worshipping congregation or any other organized form of church life. As became apparent in the case study, the centrality of the activity of God in both the story telling and in the framing of the provocative propositions dawns only gradually on the participants. Some people may want to make it much more explicit and, as it were, "public" from the start.

Whichever route is taken—that of slow discovery or instant revelation—the key issue is to ensure that prayer, worship, teaching and the process of the inquiry move hand in hand. This does not imply that every debate, every development in the inquiry has to be reported to the whole congregation and be publicly prayed over. So crass an approach can do much damage. Rather it is important to let the congregation understand that this is a process of spiritual discernment, not just a new fad from Business School.

St. Luke's achieved that, more or less, in a particular way: through the early morning prayer group, the teaching sermons on the biblical teaching on the nature of the Church, and the incorporation of some of the stories into church services. Fine. There are, however, a myriad other ways of achieving the same effect, and each church is likely to have its own particular means of expressing the same thought. Here are three caveats, culled from experience elsewhere:

1. Integrate the inquiry into the spiritual life of the church; but do not let it dominate it. Worship God, not appreciative inquiry.

2. Remember that trustfulness in God is fundamental. Don't let prayer, especially intercessory prayer, become a long nag list centered on the inquiry.

3. I address the issue of timing in the last chapter: for now, remember that a good appreciative inquiry in a medium sized congregation is likely to take some time.

So find creative ways of varying the prayer/teaching/worship component of the inquiry. Properly handled the stories can be a wonderful resource in this regard.

2. *Appreciative Inquiry or not Appreciative Inquiry? (pp. 37f)*

It should be obvious from the case study that it is important to establish an atmosphere of trustful collaboration within the whole church. This is less likely to be achieved if many members feel that an inquiry has been foisted upon them without consultation. Different churches have different methods and traditions of consultation which need to be respected. It is always sensible to give people a choice: appreciative inquiry or some other kind of intervention or nothing. If they know that they played a part in choosing appreciative inquiry, even if they have only an imperfect idea of what it involves, they are much more likely to be whole hearted and generous spirited in their response. Imposed appreciative inquiry is a contradiction in terms.

3. *Prework (pp. 34f)*

Is all this prework really necessary? Practitioners will vary in their response to that question. Some would dispense with it altogether and go right into the appreciative inquiry. I can only say that in my experience the more carefully and thoroughly the prework is done, the smoother the inquiry will go. The prework has three objectives:

❑ to begin to get the church to think creatively about itself and its patterns of life and ministry;

❑ to build up a high degree of mutual trust; and

❑ to establish in the congregation a high sense of care, compassion and God-centeredness that will enable it to undertake the spiritually demanding task of appreciative discernment in the later stages of the inquiry.

Are there any ideal forms of prework? No. The forms have to be chosen in accordance with the styles, personalities and experiences of the members of the church, and even then there is inevitably an arbitrary or random element. What works well for one group will work less well for another, and it is often very hard to tell why. Even a disaster can give everyone a good laugh, and few things bond as well as shared laughter. We find that the "social mapping" works well, because it is highly visual and it can be entirely inclusive. A variant, also borrowed from participatory rural appraisal, is to make a chart of the church's year, looking at activities, special services, involvement of different groups, impact on the local community. This builds up a sense of the seasons through the year and therefore of both continuity and change: a useful idea to implant in the collective consciousness of any group that is contemplating significant change.

4. Selecting the Work Group (pp. 40f)

This can be a bit of a minefield for the unwary. Remember that it is hard work, demanding a lot of time and some skills. People who are overcommitted already will not be able to turn up reliably, and that can have a very destabilizing and damaging effect on the work of the group, especially in the later stages of the work. At the same time, it is important to handle the relationship between the work group and the normal organs of church governance with some sensitivity; and a degree of overlap is one way of achieving that. It might be wise to enable those who join the work group to surrender other responsibilities for the duration of the inquiry.

How representative does the work group need to be? It is impossible to answer that question dogmatically, as everything depends on the social dynamics of the congregation. St. Luke's was atypical in being composed of three clear components, with a modest degree of tension between them. In that case it was necessary to include representatives of each component, and that was achieved by a voting system. In that way everyone felt doubly included: they had one (at least) of "their" sub-group on and they voted directly for all the members.

My own personal view is that we can get far too fussed about the minutiae of representation. What matters is that the people on the work group are trusted by the congregation at large; and that they are sensitive to the needs of the whole congregation. (Even if they are not at the beginning of the process, they certainly will be by the end!)

Shouldn't the church board (or its equivalent) be the Work Group? Sometimes, especially in a small church, that might be the best way forward; and sometimes the church board will decide for itself that is what it wishes. So be it. But most boards have plenty of other work to be doing while the inquiry is proceeding and it is therefore usually better to widen the circle, without allowing the church board to feel that it is being by-passed or ignored.

How big should the work group be? In the case study it was unusually small. Eight to twelve is probably ideal: there is some research that suggests that groups under seven cease to function efficiently and more to suggest that once the work group is over twelve decisions become very hard to reach. Avoid allowing the work group to be bigger than it needs to be to do the work purely as a way of placating people. That will lead to serious difficulties later.

5. The Minister or Other Church Leader Role in the Work Group or Outside It (p. 41)

In the case study Peter acted as a consultant to the work group (because he had a little previous exposure to appreciative inquiry and therefore could guide them in the sequencing) and as a channel of communication between the work group, the church board and the congregation at large. That is a very important role; arguably the most important single role of all, not least because it focuses his role on his primary task which is the leading of the prayers and worship of the whole church..

It is seldom wise for the church leader to be on the work group. He or she can too easily dominate it, even without realizing that is what is happening. More insidiously, I often find that lay people are more ready to share the kind of stories that lie at the heart of the appreciative inquiry with other lay people than with ordained ministers. Perhaps this is a special form of the fear of the expert.

It is, however, important for the minister to be close (but not over-close) to the inquiry and to be associated with it in the minds of the congregation. There is no one way of achieving this delicate balance. Approaches vary from the establishment of formal meetings with one or two members of the work group to wholly informal conversations when the opportunity offers. It is well to try to avoid the shared prayer degenerating into an information-swapping session.

What of other ordained ministers such as Sam? I was frankly surprised that Sam was on the work group. I said nothing because she was so new in the job, I did not think the usual objections I would raise were likely to stick in her case. In general, it is probably sensible to leave the work group to lay people, with the ordained ministers acting as flying buttresses, giving support from outside. I am aware that some clergy feel very threatened by exclusion, but that says much more about them and their fitness for ministry than it says about the optimal functioning of the inquiry.

6. Team building in the work group (p. 42)

Again, this is a process that some practitioners would not bother with. Our experience, however, is that the work group is likely to include—I would even say should include—people who are not well used to working together. They are going to go through a demanding, tough and spiritually-stretching process involving things they feel passionately about, and people whom they will come to love. It is surely worth spending a little time helping them, not just to get to know each other in a conventional "ice- breaker" way; but to trust and respect each other at a far deeper level. True some of that will come from their sharing of their stories as they test the appreciative protocol. More will be built up, slowly perhaps, through the experience of shared prayer which I regard as fundamental to the common life of the work group. Nonetheless, I find it helpful to work with the group for their first session or even two sessions enabling them to discover a depth of relatedness and mutual acceptance that would otherwise take a long time to develop.

There is nothing "unique" about the exercises I describe in the case study. Others will do just as well. For example, one practitioner I know gets the members to bring along a thing, an artifact, that is important to them. (Sometimes he describes it as "something you would like to be buried with you.") He then gets them to tell the story of that artifact, and in most cases people find themselves, without embarrassment, telling why that thing is so important to them. And that usually takes them into a significant moment in their lives. Another practitioner encourages people to touch each other—perhaps by blindfolding half the group, getting the other half to put their hands, or feet or hair or ear, into the hands of one of the blindfolded people, and then allowing the blindfolded to describe, in as much detail and care as they can, the limb they are holding. In as non-tactile a culture as ours, it is astonishing how powerful this exercise can be.

In the case study, the group was unusually blessed by Sam's spontaneous readiness to share some of her own burden of shame, the very reverse of the appreciative approach. That is not usual, much less mandatory. In no sense whatever, is it an objective to be aimed for. I reported it in the case study only because it happened; not because it is a pattern to be followed. It is testimony, however, to the level of spiritual centeredness that her work group had reached after the initial exercises and which thereafter enabled it to function so well.

7. *Stakeholders* (p. 47)

I need to add little on this that is not already in the text. It is, I believe, important to listen to the wider community, but it is better if the people included in the inquiry are, in however weak a sense, stakeholders in the church or other organization. The St. Luke's work group chose interviewees who had, in many cases, no real connection with the church at all, but just happened to be in easily defined roles within the community. That is not necessarily inappropriate, but it would have been preferable, at least in my view, to find people who had some connection with the church. Former members is one obvious (though sometimes delicate) category. Another is those who minister, in one sense or another, to people in the congregation. Teachers, doctors, and, yes, storekeepers may all fall into this category, but they need to be selected more intentionally than was the case in St. Luke's.

8. *Containment of the work group* (pp. 47, 55)

The work group is likely to encounter "heavy stuff" when conducting the appreciative interviews and hearing the stories. They may not be able to handle the emotional load that some of those stories imply. What do they do with those emotions? The most destructive, but also the easiest and most "natural," is to dump them on each other, with the attendant anger, hurt and confusion that such dumping brings in its train. No work group can function effectively in such a climate. Group therapists therefore talk about "holding" or "containing" this raw emotionality, rather in the way that a good mother will hold her young child's emotional responses and then allow the child to repossess just as much of them as she or he can handle.

It is highly unlikely that most church groups will have on hand a skilled facilitator who can do this for the work group. A second best solution, then, is for one member of the work group to accept responsibility for encouraging members of the group to talk about how they feel when they have heard some of the stories. Since appreciative inquiry is, at its root, an attempt to link emotional and spiritual learning with cognitive learning—how we feel to how we think—it is important both that we be aware of the feeling quality sparked by the stories; and that we are able to handle the feelings they release in us. One way of ensuring both of those is to be given space to talk about our feelings without embarrassment or a sense of intrusion.

If group members can be given space to do this, and it is likely to take time and patience for this facility to develop, a number of benefits is likely. First, the "feeling knowledge" of the group as a whole will be greatly increased. And second, the ease with which the group works together will be enhanced. More important than both of those, however, the energy and even the inspiration with which the group undertakes its primary task of enabling the church to discern its way forward under God will surprise even the members of the group. Finally it will become natural to incorporate this emotional learning in the prayer of the group. If this is done with sensitivity and compassion, it can be a rich and sustaining experience.

In St. Luke's some of this containing was done by Peter; more of it, in an almost unconscious and untutored way, by Sam, who usually led the prayers with which each meeting of the work group began and ended. With the wisdom of hindsight, I think it would have helped if I had encouraged the group to be more intentional about this; and had asked Evelyn, or any other member of the group, to accept responsibility for looking out for the emotional health of the group much earlier in the process.

9. Generative questions *(pp. 43f)*

The key to the appreciative protocol is the formulation of generative questions. Practitioners often say that the first question you ask sets the tone and even determines the outcome of the inquiry. Drafting the spirit if not the precise wording of that question—and those that follow—is thus a challenging task. So challenging, indeed, that many practitioners prefer to draft the appreciative protocol themselves, having familiarized themselves with the church or other organization by intensive discussions with as representative a sample of members and stakeholders as possible; and of course with the work group. That is certainly a way of doing it and in some circumstances it will be appropriate, especially where speed is important. My own view, however, is that it is in forming the appreciative protocol that the work group comes to own the whole process. The questions are their questions—and therefore the inquiry is their inquiry. That is not to deny an editorial or guiding role to a facilitator or consultant if one is available, but it is to insist that any work group can , with a little help and practice, produce genuinely generative questions rooted in its own experience.

The essence of generative questions is that they:

❏ generate memories, feelings and energy about the best of the past;

❏ generate interest and enthusiasm in the future;

❏ generate a sense of belonging and inclusivity;

❏ generate a sense of being taken seriously, of being accepted as a significant source of material about an important topic; and

❏ generate a response of both fact and feeling; and hold these two in a creative union.

As in the case study, I usually find that the experience of answering some generative questions that are only loosely related to the main topic of the inquiry (and which may therefore be imported from some "external" context) soon gives the members of the work group a good idea of what they are and how they work. They quickly learn that key trigger words are words such as: *best, strengths, peak, happiest, most meaningful, most holy, most spiritually significant, resources, joy, energy, wonder, dream, vision, hope, yearning, longing, delight, growth,* and *depth*. They also quickly latch on to the fact that appreciative inquiry is primarily narrative in form. It works best when the question includes an invitation to story telling: *Tell me a story about*.... In contrast it is hard to make an appreciative inquiry come alive when all the (or any of the) questions are factual or analytical in form. Questions that begin with phrases like *How many, Under what circumstances, Do you consider* are almost always heading in the wrong direction. One quick and dirty test of a generative question is to ask yourself: "If someone asked me this question about my place of work, how would I feel about answering it? Elated or dejected? High energy or low energy? Excited or bored? Pleased or sorry?" If the second of those pairs predominates, you can be pretty confident that this is not going to work as a generative question.

10. Active listening (pp. 46f)

Almost as important as asking the right questions is listening to the answers in the right way. A friend tells me that the Chinese character for "to listen" is composed of five elements: *ear, you, yes, undivided attention*, and *heart*. That says it all very beautifully. An appreciative interviewer listens with undivided attention, looking at the interviewee so he or she can empathize or feel with the person who is speaking about the deep things of the spirit.

There is only one element I would add to this ancient wisdom. Sometimes it is important to listen to what is *not* being said as well as to what is. Initially, in the first three or four interviews, that may be hard. As confidence and experience accumulate, however, one is often struck by the fact that, for example, no one is mentioning the music; or the ministers family; or the lay leadership of the church, or whatever it may be. These seem to be non-issues, or no-go areas. Such omissions may or may not be significant: nothing is more certain than that they are important bits of data that need to be fed back to the work group and checked out with them.

11. Negativities (p. 49)

An appreciative inquiry depends upon data that are emotionally satisfying. It is, furthermore, perhaps especially true of the church that people are diffident about raising issues that are painful or potentially divisive. That does not imply, however, that negativities are blanked out, suppressed or ignored. Far from it. They must not, of course, be allowed to become dominant or to lead the inquiry by the nose, and they can usually be reframed to express the appreciative. For example: "The ministers sermons are too intellectual" can be helpfully reframed as: "The sermons we find most helpful are those that are well earthed in the day to day experience of ordinary people, and expressed in the language of everyday life."

If many church-goers find it hard to talk about painful or disturbing issues and may therefore be helped to raise them by the kind of reframing illustrated above, it is also true that a very few people are only too glad to be given the chance to complain. No matter what questions are asked or how skillfully the reframing is presented, they see the inquiry as a chance to offload all their dissatisfactions. (In many cases the source of the dissatisfaction has little or nothing to do with the church, but the inquiry becomes nonetheless a convenient vehicle for giving vent to it. Almost as a by-product, the church then becomes a scapegoat.) How does the interviewer cope with such people?

If neither drawing their attention to the appreciative slant of the question; nor reframing their complaints help them move out of a negative way of talking, the only response may be to let them at least vent their negative feelings. That alone can be therapeutic. (In some circumstances it can unfortunately be the reverse.) In either case the interviewer is not there as a therapist, but as a collector of appreciative data. If there are none to be had, then cut your losses and move on, without being discourteous or inconsiderate to your interviewee.

12. Taking notes (p. 49)

As we have seen the eyes are crucially involved in active listening. That means that they should not be glued to a note pad. Equally, however, we all have finite memories, and if you are doing a lot of interviews you will inevitably find that one merges with another in your memory. Notes are vital. Here is a three pronged strategy.

1. Keep very short, simple notes as the conversation progresses.

2. If there is a particularly striking story or other comment, stop the interview and ask for permission to write more extended notes then and there.

3. As soon as the interview is over—if necessary staying in the interviewee's sitting room or wherever the conversation occurred— go through the short notes and amplify them, so that you can give a five minute report to the work group if you need to. Make especially sure that any stories you will want to report back are fully noted. Some people use portable tape recorders and then make notes at their leisure. That can be useful but my own experience is that interviewees tend to be more guarded and defensive when faced with a tape recorder. Many relax after a time, but that time could be important.

13. Confidentiality (p. 70)

Because of the nature of Christian community, it is very, very important to get this right. We find the following system works well. Everything that is said in the interview is confidential as to detail. Only broad impressions, preferences, experiences are to be revealed to anyone, and that without any tracer as to the origin of the information. However, if the interviewer is especially struck by a story or other comment (see above), permission may be sought to quote it, and the terms on which it may be quoted will be agreed (for example, is the person's name to be revealed? The time? The others involved?). Obviously, the interviewer respects the wishes of the interviewee absolutely.

Sometimes it happens that you only see the significance of a story or a piece of information later. If you want to use it in a way that would reveal its origin, you are obliged to go back and check with the interviewee. If permission to use it is refused, that refusal has, however regretfully, to be respected.

14. Trying out the appreciative protocol (pp. 46f)

This is another step that many people would miss out, and I admit it may be a little purist to insist on it. However, if you are doing a large number of interviews and especially if people other than the work group are going to be involved in doing the interviews (see below), make absolutely sure that you have debugged the protocol. To say that is not to reduce the protocol to a mechanical interview schedule: of course people will word the questions in their own ways and pack it around with their own introductory material. We are not, then, too much concerned with the word-smithing—the tyranny of the text—but we are concerned to ensure that the questions are genuinely generative. It sometimes happens that a question that ignites the work group which thought of it splutters like a damp squib when more widely applied. If you are new to this game, play safe, and try it out at least on a few people before you release it to the whole church.

15. Training additional interviewers (p. 49)

When you have decided how many additional interviewers you will need, you will have to prepare them for the task. This is not as daunting as it sounds. First, put them through the interview process themselves. That will not only give you data, but it will give them a clear idea how the interviewing process works. Then go through the mechanics of it: confidentiality, note-taking, active listening, dealing with excessive negativity, reframing. Most will understand this quite quickly, though they will need exercise with the reframing.

The next step is to give them an appreciative protocol close to but not identical with the one you are using for the inquiry and let them practice on each other. Video taping an interview can be a very powerful way of learning, especially if the instructors praise what is done well rather than highlight all the mistakes! Or you can do what Eva did in the case study and get two of the work group to simulate an interview, raising some of the important issues above.

I have kept till last the two most important aspects of the training of the interviewers. The first is to nourish their confidence: in themselves, in the process and in the team as a whole. The second is to help them to integrate their faith with their interviewing. They are setting out to hear what God is doing among his people. They need to bring to the interview, then, an expectation that God is waiting to meet them in the story of the interviewee. To put it like this is not to encourage a sloppy or sentimental lack of rigor and engagement in inquiry; but it is to insist that what we hear is heavily influenced by what we expect to hear. If we expect to hear the story of God's dealing with his people, there is a good chance that we shall do so. If we expect nothing, we are in danger of hearing nothing.

16. Is there a continuing role for the interviewers? *(pp. 51f)*

This is a question that has to be decided in every particular context. There is no uniquely right solution. In the case study, I discouraged the work group expanding itself to include all the additional interviewers for two reasons: I was worried about the work group becoming too big; and I was conscious that the "containment" of the work group was already barely adequate. In general, my own initial position is that the work group needs to learn from the interviewers as much as it can, but that does not imply that all the interviewers becoming members of the work group. I recognize that cases vary. A pragmatic but informed judgment has to be made.

17. Finding the themes *(pp. 52f)*

Sometimes the themes stick out like cacti in the desert and there is no need to make a big deal about finding them. More often, there is need for careful sifting of the data that come up from the interviews. The danger here is that the work group lapses into group-think or lowest common denominator type thinking. Again the emphasis needs to be firmly on the work of God in the church with the capacity to surprise, to take in the flank, to do the unexpected which is such a characteristic of the God of Exodus and the God of Bethlehem. Finding the themes can sometimes be the center point of the discernment with all the ambiguity, openness and slow distillation of meaning that entails. Prayerful wrestling with the data; attentive, expectant listening to the stories; spotting where the energy of the people and the purposes of God seem to cohere in something that has a significance beyond itself—all this is involved. And even this is inadequate to express what is central: the uncovering of God's work among his people.

There is, therefore, no one technique, for at this point technique breaks down or becomes redundant. We usually find, however, that getting the themes of the most gripping stories on to a wall chart begins to reveal loose patterns. Stories that superficially sound quite different are found to have more in common than is at first sight apparent. Slowly there emerges a shape, a set of ideas, directions, hopes that can be fashioned into the beginning of a provocative proposition. This is hard work: hard intellectually, hard spiritually. It is both left brain and right brain. It is analysis and poetry. It is obedience and prophecy; law and gospel.

It is usually at this point that the work group is most vulnerable to its own divisions and pathologies. It can become too dependent upon its own "leader" and if it has not yet had one, it is at this point that it might "create" one, in the hope that he or she will "save" them. Or it can slip into "blaming" mode: blaming the people, blaming each other, blaming the minister, blaming God. That this is the antithesis of the appreciative approach hardly needs saying, but that very fact merely serves to make the blaming more subtle, more subterranean, but no less real.

Whatever latent pathology the group is prey to, two counter-effects are crucial. The first is continuing prayer: within the group certainly, but also by people outside the group. In the case study, Peter's early morning prayer group, tiny and, in the world's terms, pathetic as it was, played a key role in "holding" the work group at this potentially awkward time. The work group's decision to go on retreat, to "sit with the material under the eyes of God," as one member put it, is another example. The second counter-effect is the containment of the group's anger, frustration, sense of loss, fear and anxiety in the way I have already discussed—by allowing it to surface, to be acknowledged and, as it were, laid on the table where its reality is accepted but its power to dominate is broken.

If the group is lucky enough to have a professional facilitator, he or she can ensure that this happens in a controlled and healthful way without being unnecessarily "heavy" or solemn about it. In the absence of a facilitator, one member of the group can take responsibility for asking people to express their own feelings, perhaps at the end of each session, and summarize how the group as a whole is experiencing the feeling quality of other people's stories.

18. Provocative propositions *(pp. 60f)*

As the case study brought out, provocative propositions need to be provocative! There are two issues here that need to be kept separate: language and substance. Often the language used in a proposition can sound banal, even pious, yet the reality that lies under the language is dynamite. Now non-threatening language has its strategic importance in enabling people who have not been through all the prior work to buy into the conclusions. Against that has to be set, however, the fact that such language can take the edge off the reality at which it points, especially in the longer term. If the provocative proposition is establishing a sense of direction or priority for years ahead, it is important that it communicate the energy, the longing, the excitement of spiritual discovery that gave it birth. Otherwise it will be too easily ignored once the dust settles.

The other issue is substance. A highly anxious group is unlikely to generate genuinely provocative propositions, which is one more reason why the prayerfulness and the containment of the group are both so significant. The ideal provocative proposition will feel just beyond the grasp of the church as a whole, and that means that it will seem well beyond the grasp of the more anxious, conservative or reluctant-to-change members. Sometimes church work groups feel that they need to take account of the reservations of that "tail" of the membership and tone down the scale of provocation accordingly. That is always a pity. As we shall see below, there will be times when the more anxious members have to be helped to overcome their anxiety and move forward. That is not achieved by backing off the vision the Spirit has enabled the work group to glimpse. The work group has to find the courage to be true to what it has been enabled to envision, and trust the grace of God, at work in the church as a whole, to operate with that.

19. The physical expression of the provocative propositions (pp. 71f)

In the case study, the work group at St. Luke's decided to encourage the church members to get inside the provocative propositions by modeling them, making them physically present. That will not be everyone's way. Yet many practitioners find that there is great value in the physical representation of the main provocative propositions that a church, or any other organization, commits itself to. The objective is not just to refresh the memory, important though that can be. It is also to rekindle the sense of the presence and purpose of God among his people and thus to reignite the energy and excitement that the original inquiry inflamed.

The well known Dutch practitioner, Joep de Jong, for example, always has an artist make a sketch of the provocative propositions and then Joep formally presents those sketches to the organization in the hope and expectation that they will be prominently displayed somewhere where everyone sees them everyday.

Another idea is to have a special service on the anniversary of the appreciative inquiry in which the propositions are "represented," probably accompanied by the retelling of some of the stories that triggered them. Of course the church will move on; what seemed a radical new departure two years ago has now become part of the routine. Nonetheless, the collective memory of what it felt like to commit ourselves to this project or this way of doing things can prevent the routine becoming stale or too comfortable. It is not for nothing that in many Christian traditions the central act of worship is a reenactment of the most precious memory of the church. We need representation—making present again—to keep us on track.

20. *Building consensus* (pp. 70f)

Building consensus round the provocative propositions may be a relatively formal process, as it was at St. Luke's, or it may be much less structured. I am always reluctant to get into the business of voting, because it tends to lead to a lowest common denominator result, and sometimes leaves a bitter after taste to boot. Whether the torpedo-card, used at St. Luke's, is a good idea will be contested by some practitioners, mainly for the same reason. It can too easily lead to the elimination of the novel, unconventional, high-risk ideas. (That is the theory. I have to say that in my experience it does not in practice have that result.)

What most of us find is that people need a long time to "get inside" provocative propositions, and that hurrying that process is always a bad mistake. It is hard for the work group at this point. They know this stuff inside out; they have worked it through thoroughly over an extended period. Now they want the validation of the whole church, and they cannot understand why it is all taking so long! It takes rare spiritual maturity to commend the process to God and leave the church to Him.

The role of the organs of church government—boards, councils, sessions, vestries and so on—is much debated at this point. Some churches expect their leadership, in this sense, to have prior access to the work of the inquiry and to premasticate the results before presentation to the membership as a whole. Others are content to let the church as a whole react to the results and then leave it to the church board (or whatever) to hammer the propositions into action plans in accordance with the perceived wishes of the church. This is partly a matter of ecclesiastical tradition; partly a matter of size; and partly of leadership style. I believe these to be secondary issues: the primary ones are faithfulness to the data; inclusiveness; and the courage to envision the future. If those are protected, the details of leadership-congregation relationships can be honored as tradition demands.

21. Reality checking (pp. 74f)

Provocative propositions are vision statements. If the discernment has been done prayerfully and with integrity, they have a rather special quality. They are not "revelations," but they are not just bits of paper either. They represent the best the church can now do in terms of aligning itself with what it perceives of the will of God. That does not, however, mean that questions of feasibility, practicality and change-management become irrelevant. If anything, it means that those questions need ever more careful handling.

Although it can become unwieldy with very large numbers—say over 1,000—one technique we have sometimes used is to ask members of the church, during the consensus building process, to scale the provocative propositions in terms of their innovativeness and their feasibility. The "perfect" provocative proposition will be high on innovativeness and fairly high, but not very high, on feasibility. If everyone thinks it is easily feasible, they are not being stretched. And if no one thinks it is in the least feasible, it will probably never get done! (If everyone thinks a proposition is both very feasible and not very innovative, the work group probably needs to have another look at it. For it can hardly be said to have provoked anyone.)

22. Celebration

By the time the work group has produced the provocative propositions; the congregation (or other organization) has validated them and the action plans have been prepared, a great deal of work has been done. Much has been learned. More has been shared. Many, many people have a quite different perspective on the ways of God with his people. The organization has moved far beyond its original expectation. That is cause for celebration. Celebrate it.

Chapter 10

Final Questions

In this chapter we must address two final questions that will almost certainly be in the mind of any reader who has continued this far: (1) How long will it take? and (2) Can we do it by ourselves? I shall try to answer each of those questions in turn.

First, how long will it take? Immediately you will see that is like asking how long is a piece of string. So much depends on how big the congregation or other organization is; how frequently the work group can meet; how well its members work together; how readily a consensus is built around the provocative propositions and so on, that I shudder to be over-dogmatic. All I can do is to offer some rough guidelines.

It may come as a surprise, in view of all that I have written thus far and especially in the light of the experience of St. Luke's to hear that most people are astonished at how quickly an appreciative inquiry can, under certain conditions, be completed. When working with business groups, we often find that we have been given two days. Sure, that is usually with a specific staff group of maybe twenty or thirty people and the issue is normally precisely determined before we start. (And we fight hard for a third or fourth day!) These may be rare conditions in most church settings, but I start by mentioning it to dispel the impression that may have been created that appreciative inquiry is a clumsy and time consuming tool that takes for ever to reach any conclusion. That is not the case.

Let's have a look at a time budget for two very different settings: a small rural congregation of about 80 members; and a large urban-based parachurch organization of five thousand. We will break the process down into its simplest components and see how long it would be realistic to allow for each.

1. Deciding on an appreciative inquiry in a way that allows most people feel that they have been genuinely consulted.

a. The rural church. There is no reason why this should take more than one or at the most two evenings. If it is allowed to last much longer, there is a danger that people will get bored or irritated.

b. The parachurch organization. Much will depend on how it is organized internally and how smoothly communications flow between the component parts of the organization. Further, in a very large organization like this it may not be necessary to consult the whole membership, since many will have little interest in organizational issues. In such a case, where the consultation process is limited to those actually involved in the administrative and executive life of the organization, one might be thinking of consulting something under 500 people. That is still quite a task, especially if it is to be done through some kind of dialogue or interactive process that encourages real feed back and participation. Let's leave aside computer-based forms of interaction, so that one has a choice between using existing forms of participation (for example, departmental, unit or cell meetings) or setting up some consultative process especially for this task. In the former case, the time a decision takes to emerge will depend on the frequency of meetings at the relevant level and the skill with which those meetings are run.

If one goes the other, specially designed, route, one is thinking of a number of well prepared meetings for groups that might number anything between fifty and two hundred. To organize, hold and digest the content of anything up to ten of such meetings is clearly something that cannot be done fast, no matter how well run the place may be; or how freely the leadership delegates authority. Realistically one ought to allow a minimum of a month and perhaps a maximum of two months.

In the case of St. Luke's, the "prework," between the decision to go ahead with the inquiry and its actual launch, proved valuable - e.g. the social mapping and the pairing exercises. In a small group this is not difficult to arrange and need take very little time. In a very large organization, however, it is probably true that the prework is even more important, and yet it is undeniably more demanding both conceptually and organizationally.

In the case of our imaginary parachurch organization, it would be sensible to splice some prework on to the mass meetings that we have supposed will be held to decide on whether to go ahead with an appreciative inquiry since it is costly and complicated to get everyone together. In this case the prework needs to be designed in such a way as will serve all the interventions under discussion. All such possibilities will benefit from people being enabled to think of the life of the organization as the locus of God's work among his people. This is so central a leitmotif of the kind of inquiry posited in this book that any technique of inquiry is likely to benefit from having its salience raised in the consciousness of the participants. This is not the place to describe such prework in detail, for it can only be designed in context; but variants of the wall of wonder may well be found to have wide application.

2. *Choosing the work group.*

One way of saving time is to combine this step with the first, so that one is not only asking people whether they want to go ahead with an appreciative inquiry (or a Future Search or Open Space or Skills Inventory or whatever) but, if they do, who they would like to be part of the work group that will run it. (Many of the other interventions that might be considered along with appreciative inquiry will also need some kind of responsible group, so one is no sense anticipating the outcome by planning to ask this question along with the more general procedural one of which technique to use.)

If the decision is made to keep the two issues separate, and for the sake of simplicity that might be wise, then the time budget would be like this:

a. The rural congregation: perhaps one evening to choose the work group.

b. In the parachurch group, again limiting the involvement to the "core" 500 and again relying on some interactive process within the existing administrative structures (rather than, say, a postal ballot), the process will certainly take a month and could take longer if the key administrative groups meet infrequently.

3. Getting the work group to function as a team and deciding on the generative questions.

Apart from the fact that the work group for the parachurch organization is likely to be somewhat (but not too much) bigger than the rural congregation's, the only major difference is that the latter is likely to be easier to get to work as a team, with the critical issue of trust well established, than the former where the very size of the organization is likely to result in people not knowing each other well and therefore needing time to come to trust each other. Let's allow one evening for the rural congregation, and two half days for the parachurch organization.

Once the work group starts the "real" work on the generative questions, the discrepancy between the time needed may well decrease markedly. So how long does it take? Our experience is that once a group gets the hang of the generative questions the production of their own questions takes very little time, though boiling down the suggestions to the "best" four or five may take a little longer. Let's allow a couple of sessions of the work group for that, noticing that how long that takes in calendar time will depend on how often the work group can meet, and that will depend in part on the commitment of its members.

Pretesting the protocol on a small sample of the "target" population will take little time, but tweaking the questions in the light of the results of the pretest may require the whole of one session.

Thus far we have used only three sessions of the work group, once it has shaken down. Now we are ready to train the interviewers.

4. Training the interviewers.

The big difference between the groups is that the parachurch organization is going to have to train far more interviewers, if it is to include all its members, than is the rural congregation. (Indeed the latter may decide not to train any and to leave it to the work group to interview all 80 member-families.) However, it is does not take much longer to train 50 than 5: the key issue is the skill and level of preparation of the trainers. The content of the training is not complicated; much more significant is the establishment of confidence. That usually comes from experience, and again it takes no longer for three couples to interview each other than it does for 25 couples.

However, if the parachurch organization is going to include all 5000 members, it is going to have to train about 250 interviewers. This implies five training sessions with 50 people: not a small task, certainly, but once a format is established, the process can be rolled out as often as necessary. How long it will all take obviously depends on how soon interviewers can be selected and convened.

There is of course no reason why the training of the interviewers should not start as soon as the work group is chosen: indeed the interviewers could be selected at the same time as the work group. By doing both tasks simultaneously, in parallel as it were, significant time savings can be made. Even with a large operation like the parachurch body, we might expect the work group to have produced the protocol, pretested it and trained the interviewers within a month, providing the patterns of work allow training sessions of 250 people, scattered across the organization, to be convened and conducted in so short a space.

5. *Doing the Interviews.*

a. The rural congregation has around 70 interviews to conduct and we assume around ten people to do them. If each interview lasts about forty-five minutes and the writing-up at least another forty-five, the total time commitment for all the interviews is around ten and a half hours per interviewer. It will naturally depend upon how much time each interviewer can make available, but it would not be unreasonable to expect the interviews to be done in around two weeks: a month would be the maximum.

b. The case of the large parachurch organization is not as different as you might suppose. There we have notionally allowed 250 interviewers to cover 5,000 members. That is twenty interviews per interviewer. That is quite a load, but should be doable within six to eight weeks. Over the latter period it is less than three interviews a week, hardly an over demanding striking rate.

6. *Reading the data.*

a. The small congregation can proceed in much the same way as the work group at St. Luke's, with each member of the work group reading between a quarter and a half of all the interviews. Even forty interviews is not very much and so the reading phase is not going to take long. Agreeing the themes will not usually be difficult or time consuming unless the work group begins to fracture along ideological or theological lines, a reversal made the less likely if the team building has been done properly. It would not, I believe, be unrealistic to think of a work group beginning to work on the provocative propositions within two weeks of the end of the interviewing, and perhaps having agreed propositions to put to a wider audience a week or two later, assuming that the work group is prepared to meet for a couple of fairly long and intense evenings a week.

b.   The parachurch organization has a much larger and more demanding task with a work group only fractionally bigger than that of the small congregation. There is no realistic alternative to using a computer-based content analysis program to search the interviews for common themes. That is the easy part. The more difficult, and time consuming part, is training the people who will read a significant sample of the interviews in order to preselect the phrases, words or ideas that the computer is to search for. (I am assuming that this is done manually rather than by the computer itself. There are many content analysis programs on the market that will enable the computer to search for the most frequently used phrases or words and in some applications this can be helpful. We have not found it so in this case and recommend that the identification of search topics be done "manually.") This is quite a sophisticated task, and at least some members of the work group will have to be prepared to work with the "readers" in order to guide them in the selection process.

Indeed, one method is to have the work group do the selection themselves, on the basis of having read, say, a 10% sample of all the interview reports. Certainly it is highly desirable that the work group should immerse themselves in the interview material; for that is where the gold of the appreciative inquiry lies hidden. And the danger always is that the essentially mechanical reading that is implied in a computerized content analysis will miss some of the best of the gold. (Computers are still remarkably unintelligent animals.)

Indeed so unintelligent are they that their use should be paralleled by other mechanisms for putting the work group on to some of the most gripping of the interviews. A simple way to do that is to ask all the interviewers to select the one (or two) interviews that they think point most creatively to the solutions for which the organization is looking. These may not be the best interviews in terms of brilliance or articulation or insight; but they may have just that spark of the unexpected, the creative, that leaves the reader with a strong sense of "Ah-hah!" If you decide to use the interviewers in this way, as a kind of prescreen or bloodhound, don't forget that you will need to include that in their training; and that this part of the training will need unusually careful planning, and, probably, plenty of time.

Let's assume that the parachurch organization's interviewers have highlighted about 500 interview reports that they think the work group should read; and that the work group agrees to take upon itself the task of picking up key ideas, words and phrases to be included in the content analysis. It would be reasonable to budget about three to five weeks for that; and maybe another two to three weeks to complete the scanning and analysis of the reports (assuming that this is another task that has to be fitted in around other work demands. If it is contracted out to professionals, one would look for a much faster turn round time.)

Once this phase of the work is complete, the group should have a very good idea of the key themes that are emerging and be ready to begin to move to the formation of provocative propositions. Oddly this may take not much longer than the tiny rural congregation, for the basic processes of discerning the work of God among his people are identical. (And the spiritual work of prayer and reflection which the St. Luke's people did so faithfully may vary in terms of form and style, but the time to be allocated will not change much whatever the size of the organization.)

Much the same may be said of the task of forming the provocative propositions. What matters here, in terms of the time budget, is not the size of the organization nor even the complexity of the task ahead, but the ease of working relationships within the group. A work group that is divided and becoming distrustful may take longer to reach genuinely and helpfully provocative propositions for a tiny church than a work group that is harmonious and focused on its primary task in an organization of thousands of people.

We will assume the work group of the parachurch organization is of the latter variety (and is well supported by the prayers of its members) and, fitting its meetings around the normal business of the organization, can therefore frame its provocative propositions within a couple of weeks of coming to terms with the data.

7. Building Consensus around the Provocative Propositions.

a. With such a small group, it should not be difficult to establish a consensus around the provocative propositions in the course of one or two meetings, if but only if the provocative propositions are reflecting back to the group their own best experiences and hopes. Or, to put it another way, consensus is the more easily built around even tough and demanding ultra-provocative propositions if people recognize them as enshrining at least some elements of their own realities, both present and future. If on the other hand the provocative propositions strike people as being off the wall, divisive, wholly impractical or absurd, building a consensus around them will be, and should be, next to impossible, no matter how long you take. This suggests a rule of thumb. If consensus comes very quickly and easily, you have not been provocative enough. If it never comes or has to be forced by resort to crude majority-seeking, you may have gone too far in the opposite direction.

b. Consensus building in a huge organization like the parachurch body is bound to be slow. Haste at this point will almost certainly be counter-productive, no matter how well the work group has done its task or how smooth are personal and institutional relationships. Usually consensus is best built from the bottom up and that implies a series of small group meetings, each reporting back, either to the work group or to another cross section of the organization. When this institutional mastication has gone far enough, it may be thought wise to repeat the mass consultation process with which appreciative inquiry was selected in the first place. "You asked for an appreciative inquiry. This is what it has come up with. What do you think? Has it identified the best way forward?"

If we allow two months for the mastication and another two months for the convening of a number of mass meetings, it looks as though it would be possible to go from the initial formulation of the provocative propositions by the work group to consensus in about four months. To the "shoot from the hip" style of corporate leader that may seem eternity; but just reflect on how much has been achieved in that period in terms of the possibility of organizational transformation, and the reality of discernment of God's purposes in and through the organization. It would need a leader of rare insensitivity indeed to begrudge four months for so radical a shift in perspective.

We are now in a position to answer the question we posed at the start, given the assumptions about the smoothness of working relationships that we have had to make as we have gone along. It looks as if the rural congregation should be through the whole process in around two to three months. The very large parachurch organization will, of course, have taken a lot longer just because nearly a hundred times as many people are involved. Even so, it should be through the whole process within twelve months, and virtually everyone has been heard and feels included.

To conclude, I must emphasize what I have hinted at several times so far. Although size and complexity of the organization that is the subject of the inquiry are important features that will dictate how long it takes, they are by no means the only ones, and can give misleading guidance to those forming a time-budget. How well the work group functions, both in terms of the regularity of its meetings and, more important, the quality of interaction between the members, will have a major impact on the speed with which two critical functions are carried out: the development of the protocol and the processing of the data, leading to the formulation of the provocative propositions.

A final point on this question of time. There is an important balance to be struck between urgency and expansiveness. The work is so important that it cannot and should not be rushed; but nor should it be allowed to drift along with little sense of excitement and expectation. If we really are about helping people to discern the movement of the Spirit in their corporate lives, we will be sufficiently motivated to be a little impatient to see the results. While respecting that godly impatience, we may need to remember, too, that the things of the Spirit cannot be rushed or force-fed. The biblical images are all about seasons, about growth, about the imperceptible changes of the natural order. In a word, then, keep it moving but don't be panicked by the calendar.

Now the final question: can we do it alone or do we need a consultant to help us?

I hope I have convinced you that appreciative inquiry, in the applications we have considered here, is first and foremost a spiritual discipline, founded on prayer and reflection. Only secondarily is it a technique of research. While it would be too simplistic to say that if you can say your prayers and practice the arts of spiritual discernment in your own life, then you can conduct an appreciative inquiry, I would want to emphasize the primacy of those spiritual gifts/disciplines over any of the procedural insights a consultant might offer.

As I have stressed in slightly different contexts throughout this short book, confidence is three quarters of the issue. There are procedures and processes that have been found to be helpful, as I have set them out in these chapters, but they should never be seen as a straight jacket or a just-add-water guide to instant solutions. At the end of the day, the basic idea of appreciative inquiry, to find God in the best experiences of His people, is so simple that it hardly matters what you do—as long as you do it prayerfully, reflectively and lovingly.

Nonetheless we recognize that people do need encouraging, giving confidence in their own judgment and their own instincts. To that end we have set up a computer link through the *Institute of Church Leadership* so that anyone who is engaged in, or thinking of starting, an appreciative inquiry in their congregation or other Church-related institution can interact with me. (For more information see Appendix 2.)

We believe that consulting over the Internet will be sufficient support for the vast majority of church organizations which want to undertake their own appreciative inquiry. For the small minority of very large or unusually complex organizations for whom a "do it yourself" approach is not appropriate or feasible, we can suggest consultants and/or training opportunities through the Institute of Church Leadership, PO Box 1098, Matthews, NC 28106. We may also be able to put such organizations in touch with others who have completed an appreciative inquiry and who are willing to share the experience they have acquired.

The most common biblical injunction is "Don't be afraid." And the context in which that injunction is offered is usually that of drawing closer to God in one way or another. It therefore makes a specially fitting ending to this little book. Take it to heart.

Appendix 1

The Strategic Planning Resource Kit

This book is part of a resource kit that includes a workbook and two audio training tapes.

The workbook provides supplementary material and exercises to train members of the planning work group. Special attention is given to both collecting and interpreting interview data and information. Each member of the work group should have a personal copy of the *Planning Workbook*. The price is $5 per book.

In the audio training tapes Charles Elliott personally walks the listener through the entire appreciative planning process as reflected in this book. These tapes enable church leaders and work group members to gain a better perspective of what appreciative inquiry is all about, and how the appreciative planning process unfolds in the life of a congregation. The price for the two tapes is $19.95.

These resources may be ordered from Christian Ministry Resources by calling 1-800-222-1840.

LINCOLN CHRISTIAN COLLEGE AND SEMINARY

Appendix 2

Consulting with the Author

Charles Elliott is available as a consultant for churches and para-church organizations which intend to use an appreciative approach to planning. He or one of his immediate colleagues may be available to visit organizations intending to launch an appreciative inquiry. Alternatively, his consulting services can be offered via the Internet, enabling church leaders to interact with Dr. Elliott at a modest cost.

Those desiring to engage Dr. Elliott as a consultant may contact him using e-mail at the following Internet address:

113173.145@compuserve.com

or write to him in care of the publisher using the following address:

Dr. Charles Elliott
c/o Christian Ministry Resources
PO Box 2301
Matthews, NC 28106.

254
EL46

LINCOLN CHRISTIAN COLLEGE AND SEMINARY

95297

3 4711 00097 4354